The Language of Evil

Guy Doza

The Language of Evil

How Dictators Manipulate the Masses and
Wield Power Through Words

Guy Doza

Canbury Press

First published by Canbury Press 2025

This edition published 2025

Publisher: Canbury Press (www.canburypress.com)

14 Beresford Rd, London, KT2 6LR, United Kingdom

EU Authorised Representative: Easy Access System Europe

- Mustamäe tee 50, 10621 Tallinn, Estonia, gpsr.requests@easproject.com

Printed and bound in Czechia by Finidr

Typeset in Athelas (heading), Futura PT (body)

All rights reserved © Guy Doza

Guy Doza has asserted his right to be identified

as the author of this work in accordance with Section 77

of the Copyright, Designs and Patents Act 1988

This is a work of non-fiction

FSC® helps take care of forests for future generations.

ISBN:

Hardback 9781914487057

Ebook 9781914487279

Contents

Introduction	9
1. Julius Caesar	17
2. Attila the Hun	31
3. Wu Zetian	45
4. Chinggis Khan	55
5. The Queens of Europe	69
• Isabella I of Castile	69
• Mary I	75
• Elizabeth I	83
6. Napoleon Bonaparte	89
7. Ranavalona I	103
8. Mussolini	117
9. Joseph Goebbels	135
10. Adolf Hitler	151
11. Joseph Stalin	167
12. Eva Perón	179
13. Jiang Qing	191
14. Mobutu	205
15. Indira Gandhi	217
16. Saddam Hussein	229
Conclusion	241
Glossary of Rhetorical Terms	245
List of Illustrations	251
Acknowledgements	263

I would like to dedicate this book to all the teachers:
past, present, and future.

INTRODUCTION

'Cry Havoc!' and let slip the dogs of war!'

Over the corpse of the recently murdered Julius Caesar in Shakespeare's *Julius Caesar*, Mark Antony calls for havoc – widespread chaos and destruction.

Compare this order to the closing sentence used by Joseph Goebbels to end his infamous '*Total War*' speech in 1943: 'Now, people rise up and let the storm break loose!' Goebbels, the Nazi's notorious Minister of Propaganda, tells his audience to unleash their anger, to rampage and kill.

Both of these examples urge the audience to embrace frenzy and go to war. Both were successful. In the play *Julius Caesar*, Mark Antony convinced his audience to take arms. In Nazi Germany, Goebbels received monstrous roars of approval from his German audience, having made the case for 'total war'.

Both examples are imperative sentences taken from the end of a speech. Both used a metaphor of power and destruction. Both incited riot and chaos from their feral audiences. Coincidence? Sadly not. This is the strategic application of the Language of Evil.

Throughout history, across different languages, irrespective of time and place, whether in literature or real life, dictators and their allies – the villains and tyrants of history – have consistently reused the same rhetorical patterns. From the cerebral Julius Caesar to the marauding Mongolian Chinggis Khan, from the silver tongue of China's Wu Zetian to Madagascar's bloodthirsty Queen Ranavalona; from the communist Joseph Stalin to the fascist Adolf Hitler, all used rhetoric to control the masses. From rallying war speeches to oppressive edicts, the most powerful and influential tyrants always seem to know what to say and how to say it in order to achieve their ends.

Together, we will journey into their world of words: words of malice, control, and power. If you ever wanted to know how evil people think, how they formulate their words, how they wield their power through rhetoric, then read on.

What is Rhetoric?

Let's start at the beginning, first. What is rhetoric? Put simply, rhetoric is the art of persuasion. Some might argue that persuasion is too kind a word for this glib art and would prefer to call it the magic of manipulation. Either way, rhetoric refers to the *language* we use to change the world around us – for good or bad.

If a person uses a certain pattern of repetition to emphasise a key point to inspire their audience to take some sort of action, they are using rhetoric; if someone uses emotive words that tug on our heartstrings, they are using rhetoric; if someone repeats the opening and closing parts of their sentences in a triadic structure, they are using rhetoric.

Even toddlers realise that certain words are more effective for making things happen than others. It could simply be that artificially elongated nagging 'please' that children use to manipulate their parents into letting them stay up late. So, whether you are a tyrannical leader trying to instil the fear of God into their audience or a toddler nagging for ice cream, we all use rhetoric.

The essence of all human language and communication is persuasion. And that persuasion, whether we realise it or not, is underpinned on a foundation of rhetoric.

Today, rhetoric is commonly used to describe language we disapprove of. The media, for instance, use rhetoric to describe disliked politicians and regimes. Rhetoric has a connotation of insincerity. This is nothing new. In Shakespeare's time, people viewed rhetoric as the art of deceit. In *King Lear*, the mad king asks each of his daughters how much they love him so that he can decide how to divide his kingdom between them. After listening to her sisters' grovelling declarations of love, his youngest daughter Cordelia says: 'If for I want the glib and oily art, To speak and purpose not'. She is describing rhetoric. While rhetoric can be glib and oily, it isn't always so.

Rhetoric had a better reputation in times long gone. Indeed, the rules of rhetoric and the terms to identify the individual components were labelled thousands of years ago by the Greek philosopher Aristotle and the Roman statesman Cicero – the ancient forefathers of the persuasive arts. Even though these techniques were identified and labelled all those years ago, their existence in literature predates our Ancient Greco-Roman classifications.

So why is rhetoric so effective? Some say that it is because rhetoric taps into an innate part of human psychology. Others claim it works because it has been around so long and is so deeply rooted in our linguistic heritage. Perhaps, it is a combination of both. Whatever the reason, the words we use and the way we use them have, for thousands of years, shaped the course of history.

The Ethics of Rhetoric

Being good at rhetoric does not make a person good at other things – for example, being a humane person. In fact, some of the most eloquent and powerful orators have been some of the most detestable people. Their words have been responsible for evil. So why should we look at these words? Why should we revisit the cruel language which led to genocides: the words that eradicated villages, incentivised murder, and attempted to trigger – and then justify – the greatest atrocities of history?

Some will argue that we need to study this evil so that we don't fall prey to it again – they argue that through studying history we prevent it from repeating itself.

On the other hand, others will argue that by dabbling in the rhetoric of evil we risk opening it up to resurface back into the world – allowing it to once more take its grip on humanity. They claim that it is safest to leave it hidden in the darkest unvisited corners of history.

I have no intention of unleashing some great evil, but I do want to highlight how language can change the way we think and act and, thus, improve the future identification of would-be tyrants.

There is something about the human condition that makes humans particularly weak when faced with a powerful speech. When I say weak, I mean logically. When we hear a masterful speaker deliver a powerful speech, our reasoning is swayed and our logic distorted. The power of the spoken word over an individual's thinking is unparalleled. Through studying these speeches we can understand that process better.

Speeches have a way of altering the way we think. And the way we think dictates the conclusions we draw; the decisions we make; the people we become. In essence, when we hear certain speeches, we become different people. The English philosopher Francis Bacon suggested that people prefer to believe what they prefer to be true. But what if... what we prefer to be true can be changed?

Sometimes speeches make us sad, sometimes angry, and sometimes they ignite a burning desire for justice. I am not exaggerating when I say that speeches have literally put audiences – human beings with lives, families, and pets – into a bloodthirsty frenzy. What is it about the human condition that makes us so vulnerable to the spoken word?

When well delivered, the spoken word harnesses the power of emotion. The spoken word is always more emotional than the written. An effective speaker takes their audience on a journey filled with different emotions: emotions they will experience live. In a room with hundreds or thousands of other people, this phenomenon magnifies the effects of the speaker. When we are processing our response to emotions in the heat of a speech, we don't scrutinise the logic behind that message and are therefore more likely to be indoctrinated – especially when we're carried away by the cheers of the audience. Our emotions deceive us into believing something that we otherwise wouldn't necessarily agree with. Some speakers ride the waves of public emotion whereas others create them. And waves, when they're big enough, can be truly destructive.

Some will argue that if an audience doesn't know how rhetoric works – how slippery and deceptive it can be – they are more prone to its effects. Certainly, persuasion works best on an unsuspecting audience. The more you learn about rhetoric, the more suspicious you become. The more suspicious you become, the less rhetoric works. It is easier to trick a fool than a scholar.

As a social phenomenon, speeches are probably the closest thing we get to an echo chamber. Ideas reverberate and ricochet off the walls and ceilings, through the microphones and the applause, the chanting and the cheering, creating a cacophony which deafens logic and blinds reasoning. To use Hitler's own words:

> [when a person] steps for the first time into a mass meeting and has thousands and thousands of people of the same opinions around him, when, as a seeker, he is swept away by three or four thousand others into the mighty effect of suggestive intoxication and enthusiasm, when the visible success and agreement of thousands confirm to him the rightness of the new doctrine and for the first time arouse doubt in the truth of his previous conviction – then he himself has succumbed to the magic influence of what me might designate as 'mass suggestion.

The Nazis were very much aware of the 'magic' of rhetoric.

If we agree that rhetoric can manipulate the thoughts and ideas of an audience, we then find ourselves in an ethical conundrum: does a speaker's eloquence exonerate an audience's acceptance of their ideas? To use an extreme example, Hitler and his regime of Nazis managed to whip up their German audience into a frenzy. Does their ability to effectively deliver a well-written speech imply the innocence of the German people who supported them? The answer is no.

Indoctrination does not justify crime. Perhaps the audience lost sight of their humanity due to stupidity (they were unable to properly comprehend the ideas that they embraced), or perhaps they were just nasty people. Whatever reason you ascribe to them, the supporters of Hitler and Nazism were guilty of a historical crime.

I hope that in reading this book you learn of the vulnerability of the human mind and the power of the spoken word – and how the combination of the two has frequently altered the course of history for the worse.

Julius Caesar (100 BC-44 BC).
Portrait by Peter Paul Rubens, oil on panel, c.1625/6.

1.
JULIUS CAESAR

One of the most famous historical figures, Caesar was born in 100 BC to a minor noble family. He managed to rise through the ranks of the Ancient Roman elite and became the most powerful Roman that ever lived. As well as invading Britain and extending Rome's reach to the corners of Egypt, France, and Belgium, Caesar conquered huge swathes of the Mediterranean, from Turkey to Spain, making Rome the most powerful Republic the world had ever seen.

Determined, eloquent, and versatile, Caesar was variously a politician, lawyer, and general. In 49 BC, he was appointed Dictator, an official fixed-term position in the Roman government that granted powers to resolve serious matters of state. In 44 BC, Caesar promoted himself further to *Dictator Perpetuo* (Dictator for Life).

While Caesar is famous for his feats on the battlefield, what is less well known is that he was an accomplished orator. Contemporary sources tell us of his linguistic dominance, though not much of what he said survives. Perhaps this intellectual omission exists because the study of Ancient Roman speeches is dominated by Cicero: a Roman senator who made a point of writing down grand speeches in which he victoriously managed to sway an audience.

While Cicero is commonly seen as the master of Roman rhetoric, the history books tell a slightly different story. The Ancient Roman historian, Suetonius, wrote, 'in eloquence [...] he [Caesar] equalled at least, if he did not surpass, the greatest of men' – a strong allusion to the possibility that Caesar was possibly even better at public speaking than Cicero. Suetonius goes on to say that even Cicero admitted that Caesar, 'had an elegant, splendid, noble, and magnificent vein of eloquence'.

The reason that Cicero is celebrated as the famous orator and Caesar is not, is that most of what Caesar said was lost, while Cicero's speeches remain. No one remembers what Caesar said and, if anyone wrote it down, the texts no longer exist. Cicero, on the other hand, documented, glorified, and potentially dramatised his speeches to the point where his rhetorical brilliance dominated history: and continues to do so to this day.

Some Problems

The few speech fragments we do have of Caesar's are in his native Latin. When approaching a text in translation we risk losing an element of the composition. The spoken word thrives on rhythm, pace, and assonance: all of which are lost, either partially or completely, when translated from one language to another. Fortunately, a lot of rhetoric survives translation, which gives the modern reader an understanding of how these speeches were constructed.

The second problem, which is especially true of ancient speakers, is that there is often a lack of reliable sources to verify their historical truth. For example, most of Caesar's speeches exist either as fragments or testimonials which were written down by later historians, many of whom were writing long after his death and with their own biases and agendas. While the surviving speeches are almost certainly not historically accurate, they do, nevertheless, give a strong indication of how people thought dictators spoke when the primary sources were written. This is valuable in itself. For example, even if a source was written 165 years after Caesar's death, as is the case with Suetonius, we can assume that Suetonius was informed by other sources – sources which no longer exist.

One of the most impressive speeches given by Caesar was delivered during the debate on the fate of the Catilinarian conspirators in 63 BC. Sadly, none of his words are remembered, but various ancient historians describe their formidable nature.

Caesar's Career

Caesar was probably such a powerful speaker in part because he grew up in a world where rhetoric was one of the foundations of education. As the son of a minor aristocratic family, he also had his own dedicated rhetoric tutor, a man named Marcus Antonius Gnipho, who later founded a school of public speaking frequented by Cicero.

At the age of 25, Caesar was said to be travelling to Rhodes to study oratory and master the spoken arts when one of the most famous escapades in the ancient world befell him. On the journey to Rhodes, according to *Life of Caesar,* an account by the ancient Roman historian Plutarch, the young Caesar was kidnapped by pirates. Little did the pirates know that the misfortune was theirs. Julius Caesar was their hostage for 38 days and spent a lot of that time writing and reciting speeches to captors, who were forced to listen. Plutarch tells us that when some of the pirates failed to respond with what Caesar deemed to be adequate enthusiasm, he branded them 'illiterate savages'. On hearing that they planned to ransom him for 20 talents, the young Caesar berated them and insisted he was worth at least 50. After his release, Caesar raised an army, caught up with the pirates, and had them all killed.

Caesar went on to become Rome's greatest general, a skilled lawyer and a highly successful politician. Words were arguably as important to his career as his military prowess, if not more so. How did he use them? And what rhetorical foundation did Caesar set which would be used to guide future leaders across the world?

Ethos, Logos, and Pathos

Although most of his speeches are lost to us, we can get a sense of Caesar's skilled wordplay in his funeral oration for his aunt Julia in 68 BC, long before he ruled Rome. Here, Caesar used the techniques of *ethos, logos,* and arguably *pathos* too. *Ethos, logos,* and *pathos* are considered to be the three main branches of rhetoric; the foundation stones of persuasion:

- ethos – invokes character
- logos – invokes logic
- pathos – invokes emotions

The opening words from his eulogy exist thanks to the work of the ancient historian Suetonius:

> The family of my aunt Julia is descended by her mother from the kings and on her father's side is akin to the immortal gods. For the Marcii Reges go back to Ancus Marcius, and the Iulii, the

> family of which ours is a branch, to Venus. Our stock therefore has at once the sanctity of kings, whose power is supreme among mortal men, and the claim to reverence which attaches to the gods, who hold sway over kings themselves.

In this short extract, Julius Caesar argued that his family came from a line of kings and gods. For *ethos*, nothing tends to outrank a claim to divinity in your bloodline. Throughout history, dictators repeatedly claim a connection to the divine and the supernatural, which you may notice in subsequent chapters. This is because, throughout history, people in positions with less privilege have looked up at greater people and asked: *Why are they better than us? Why do they get to wear the best clothes and eat the finest food while we wear rags and eat scraps?* Throughout history, perhaps even occasionally today, the people in power have answered those questions with a simple application of *ethos*: we are gods.

Even today, the British monarch claims to be appointed and anointed by God. That means that God has willed his privilege and to challenge that privilege is – theoretically – to challenge the will of God. At face value, this isn't too different to what Julius Caesar did back in 68 BC. Another modern example can be observed when the US President George Bush Jr reportedly said that he invaded Iraq because 'God told me to end the tyranny in Iraq'.

Invoking *ethos* through connections with the divine is also a use of logic: what the ancients called *logos*. The audience is presented with what is called a logical syllogism. A logical syllogism simply refers to an argument that is made in steps, or premises. Most basic syllogisms will have two minor premises and one conclusion. Mapped out, Caesar's argument might look like this:

Minor premise one: People who are linked to gods deserve privilege and power.

Minor premise two: I am linked to the gods.

Conclusion: Therefore, I deserve privilege and power.

Julius Caesar did not, of course, explicitly say that he deserved privilege and power. But he implied it by what he said. When a syllogism contains either an implied conclusion or an implied premise, it is known as an *enthymeme*.

Therefore, by invoking *ethos* through his divine links, Caesar also used *logos* in the form of an *enthymeme*. Arguably, every use of *ethos* to persuade an audience also has a logical foundation. Caesar would have been very much aware of the effects that his words would have had on his audience, and each word would have been carefully chosen to reinforce his own status.

When exploring Caesar's use of *pathos* in his funeral oration, the text loses some of its magic by being translated. In the original Latin, Caesar used rhythm, vocabulary, and word order that replicated the traditional Roman funeral orations, which invoked a poetic and emotional response from the audience.

The Power of Antithesis

As well as having used *ethos*, *logos*, and *pathos*, Caesar, in just this short extract, used another rhetorical feature called *antithesis*. Antithesis is the use of contrast to enhance an effect on an audience. Caesar said, 'by her mother from the kings and on her father's side is akin to the immortal gods'. With the contrasting roles of mother and father coupled up with kings and gods, Caesar emphasised his message that his greatness is all encompassing and comes from both sides. In rhetorical terms, one might say that Caesar used *antithesis* to bolster his *ethos*.

Speeches like this one paved the foundation for Caesar's glory: the grander you make yourself seem, the grander you become. It was true then, and, in many ways, is still true now.

This leads us on to an important point about the value and importance of speeches to powerful leaders. They will take any opportunity to build their reputation and get closer to achieving power. Be it a formal ceremony, an aunt's funeral, or their mother's birthday party, you can be guaranteed that they will move towards centre stage.

Commentarii de Bello Gallico

While rhetoric is more powerful when spoken by an effective orator, it can still sting in its written form. As he roamed the known world subjugatuing native peoples, Julius Caesar wrote commentaries on his battles. One of the most famous is his *Commentary of the Gallic Wars: Commentarii de Bello Gallico*, in Latin.

Here are the opening words, in Latin:

> Gallia est omnis divisa in partes tres, quarum unam incolunt Belgae, aliam Aquitani, tertiam qui ipsorum lingua Celtae, nostra Galli appellantur. Hi omnes lingua, institutis, legibus inter se differunt. Gallos ab Aquitanis Garumna flumen, a Belgis Matrona et Sequana dividit.

In English:

> All Gaul is divided into three parts, one of which the Belgae inhabit, the Aquitani another, those who in their own language

are called Celts, in ours Gauls, the third. All these differ from each other in language, customs and laws. The river Garonne separates the Gauls from the Aquitani; the Marne and the Seine separate them from the Belgae.

Ethos isn't only used for defining the character of the person using it. It can also be used to define characteristics of another person or group. Caesar used *ethos* later on in the opening sentences of his commentary when he went on to say:

> Of all these, the Belgae are the bravest

Later on in the commentary, he documented that some suggested his troops might be anxious to march into battle, and that he dismissed this claim with a great speech. Documenting his own speech in the third person, Caesar said:

> As to its being reported that the soldiers would not be obedient to command, or advance, he [Caesar] was not at all disturbed at that; for he knew that in the case of all those whose army had not been obedient to command, either upon some mismanagement of an affair, fortune had deserted them, or, that upon some crime being discovered, covetousness had been clearly proved [against them]. His integrity had been seen throughout his whole life, his good fortune in the war with the Helvetii.

Caesar told his troops that his reputation and credibility will ensure their loyalty and bravery. This is another example of him invoking *ethos* to build support.

According to his own account:

Upon the delivery of this speech, the minds of all were changed in a surprising manner, and the highest ardour and eagerness for prosecuting the war were engendered.

The Dictator's Greatest Phrase

Despite being an all-conquering military hero, Caesar was still beholden to his superiors in Rome. During this period, Rome had a democratic structure where the Senate (made up of appointed senators) held significant power and represented the people. Perhaps disgruntled by Caesar's popularity and rising fame, the Roman Senate, led by the general Pompey, ordered Caesar – likely out of jealousy or fear – to disband his army and return to Rome.

Being both popular and powerful, Caesar decided to refuse the Senate and returned to Rome with his army very much intact. In 49 BC, after years of fighting aboard, Caesar took a legion (a large army) and crossed the river Rubicon. The Rubicon was the official boundary he was not allowed to cross with his not-disbanded army. By crossing that river with his army, Caesar triggered a civil war against Pompey and the Senate: a civil war he ended up winning.

With Pompey gone, the reformed Senate appointed Caesar as dictator of Rome. The most famous words attributed to Caesar the dictator were not spoken but written in a letter. To truly understand the grandeur of these words we need to know the context in which they were delivered.

Caesar had a loyal ally called Gnaeus Domitius Calvinus, a fellow general and politician. Due to a series of unfortunate events, Domitius and his army suffered a defeat in battle against Pharnaces II, King of Pontus; a long-gone kingdom located in present-day Turkey. After successfully beating one of the many Roman armies, the King of

Pontus was stirring up anti-Roman sentiment in the region with other local princes.

On hearing of his friend's defeat, and of the braggadocious behaviour of the King of Pontus, Caesar, accompanied by three legions, marched to Pontus and, to quote Plutarch, 'annihilated' Pharnaces II's army in the Battle of Zela, leaving their king no option but to flee.

In a letter sent back to Rome, to emphasise the swiftness and fierceness of his victory, Caesar simply wrote:

Veni, vidi, vici

Translated, he said: 'I came; I saw; I conquered'.

Plutarch wrote *Life of Caesar* in Attic Greek and made a point of emphasising: 'In Latin, however, the words have the same inflection ending, and so a brevity which is most impressive'. Caesar would have been fully aware of how impressive and mighty these words made him seem. He was once more establishing his authority through the use of *ethos*.

The most striking thing to note about these three words is that they were structured into three parts. In rhetoric, this is known as a *tricolon*. A *tricolon* can be any form of repetition in three parts: it may be a single word repeated three times; an argument structured into three points; or a use of three sentences of a similar length to create rhythm. Despite perhaps sounding simplistic, *tricolons* (*trica*, if one prefers to avoid linguistic anglicisation) are the foundation of some of the most famous and memorable quotes throughout history. A *tricolon* can manifest power, precision, and poetry all at the same time.

Some say that the *tricolon* is such an effective feature because it is deeply ingrained in our linguist culture; others suggest that it is an innate part of the human condition; and some argue that three is the minimum number of beats needed to create a pattern. Whatever the reason, we can be assured that, as far as rhetoric is concerned, *tricolons* work and can be incredibly powerful.

As well as being a use of *tricolon*, Caesar's short quote is also a use of yet another rhetorical technique that we call *anaphora*. *Anaphora* is repetition at the beginning of sentences of clauses. While this is more evident with the repetition of 'I' in the English translation, the Latin grammar creates an equivalent effect.

We've touched on how *ethos* can be used with words, but these words are often part of a wider campaign of power and authority. Throughout Roman history, various emperors claimed to have divine ancestry to justify their position. Many sculptures would present emperors with larger-than-life eyes which was a well-known indication of divinity to the everyday Roman. The emperor Caligula even went as far as to put his three sisters on coins as goddesses. These coins would have travelled across the empire propagating the narrative of Caligula and his family's divine heritage. Coins were probably the closest thing the Romans had to social media. A short message was stamped on a coin and that short message was distributed to all corners of society.

Having a powerful and well-defined *ethos* is crucial to becoming a successful leader. Most tyrants and dictators strive to build a personality cult around them, and their most effective way of doing so was through words: specifically, speeches. Julius Caesar, and many dictators after him, built their *ethos* around links to the divine and the supernatural. As we can see from Caesar, *logos*, *pathos*, *antithesis*, *tricolon*, and *anaphora* are all supporting rhetorical schemes and tropes that helped him get to the top.

The End of Caesar

Caesar's newly concentrated power, however, didn't sit well with some of his former friends. Many senators were worried what this would mean for the future of the Roman Republic, so they took matters into their own hands. On 15 March 44 BC, Caesar was mobbed by a group of senators who reportedly stabbed him 23 times. Caesar, the most powerful man in the world, was dead. Rome, once more, was plunged into the chaos of civil war.

Caesar's assassination teaches us that even if you present the world with a divine *ethos*, it may not be accepted by everyone. For many dictators, the struggle is getting the right people to accept your ethos. As we shall later see, for Chinggis Khan, it was his fellow chieftains, for Napoleon, it was his soldiers, and for Queen Isabella I of Spain, it was an angry mob. *Ethos* is central to tyranny and power; and, in many cases, power begins to accumulate with an expression of authority at the right place at the right time.

Attila the Hun (c 406-453).
As shown in the Nuremberg Chronicle in 1493.

2.
ATTILA THE HUN

While Caesar had his brutal moments, he is documented in the history books as a scholar and is generally considered to fall on the 'right side' of history. Many dictators and tyrants who followed are remembered as savage destroyers who revelled in death, chaos and destruction. However, even these 'barbarians' gave skilful speeches to win favour, consolidate power, and assert *ethos*. Chief among them was Attila the Hun.

The Huns were a nomadic people from Central Asia who swept the known world in search of glory and riches. In the fifth century AD, Attila led an all-conquering army which brought the mighty Roman Empire to its knees, plundered its cities, and ransomed peace for extortionate quantities of gold.

Despite his well-deserved bloodthirsty reputation, Attila himself was recounted in one historical account as being modest in his dress and manner. In his contemporaneous account of a lunch held by Attila, the Greek historian and Eastern Roman diplomat Priscus recorded how Attila chose not to exercise the finery of his court:

> A luxurious meal, served on a silver plate, had been made ready for us and the barbarian guests, but Attila ate nothing but meat on a wooden trencher. In everything else, too, he showed himself temperate; his cup was of wood, while to the guests were given goblets of gold and silver. His dress, too, was quite simple, affecting only to be clean. The sword he carried at his side, the latchets of his Scythian shoes, the bridle of his horse were not adorned, like those of the other Scythians, with gold or gems or anything costly.

However, Attila knew the power of obedience – and the importance of being vaunted. Priscus noted:

> When the viands of the first course had been consumed we all stood up, and did not resume our seats until each one, in the order before observed, drank to the health of Attila in the goblet of wine presented to him.

Attila's Rise

Attila the Hun is thought to have been born around the turn of the 5th century: no one knows for sure, but quite a few historians say 406 AD. (Hunnic accounts of Attila's life were documented in epic poems which were passed down orally in the Hunnic language and, as one might imagine, are near non-existent and unreliable).

Contrary to popular belief, Attila was born into an elite ruling family, in what is present-day Hungary. Coming from an elite family meant that he would have received a formal education, which included, as was the case for nobles of the time, an education in rhetoric and speeches.

He and his brother Bleda inherited the Hunnic empire in 434 and ruled together until 445 when Attila's brother died. Some accounts – notably, Priscus – suggest that Bleda was assassinated by a power-hungry Attila, who wanted to rule solo:

> ...he succeeded to the throne of the Huns, together with his brother Bleda. In order that he might first be equal to the expedition he was preparing, he sought to increase his strength by murder. Thus he proceeded from the destruction of his own kindred to the menace of all others. But though he increased his power by this shameful means, yet by the balance of justice he received the hideous consequences of his own cruelty. Now when his brother Bleda, who ruled over a great part of the Huns, had been slain by his treachery, Attila united all the people under his own rule. Gathering also a host of the other tribes which he then held under his sway, he sought to subdue the foremost nations of the world—the Romans and the Visigoths.

Theodosius II, emperor of the Eastern Roman Empire, was regularly tormented by Attila the Hun. Attila forced the Eastern Roman Empire to pay an annual tribute of 700 pounds of gold in exchange for peace: a huge amount of money at the time. Claiming that Theodosius II broke the agreement by underpaying the tribute, Attila resumed his raids on Eastern Roman towns, with large forces ravaging settlements along the Danube – Hunnic forces even went as far as capturing and destroying the city of Serdica (present-day Sofia, capital of Bulgaria). After once more humiliating the Eastern Roman empire in battle, Attila forced the empire to sign a new peace treaty with an extortionately higher annual tribute of 2,100 pounds of gold a year.

Theodosius II was forced to accept these outrageous terms because he had no other choice.

Often referred to as *Flagellum Dei* (the Scourge of God), Attila was feared by his enemies and allies alike. While his relationship with the Eastern Roman Empire was turbulent, his relationship with the Western Roman Empire was relatively amicable towards the beginning of his reign.

Then Attila got bored, horny, and power-hungry. The emperor of the Western Roman Empire, Valentinian III, was not impressed when Attila the Hun sent ambassadors to declare that he intended to marry his sister, Justa Grata Honoria, and demanded huge swathes of the Western Roman Empire as a dowry payment. Shortly after Valentinian III refused to hand over his sister, Attila invaded Roman Gaul: a key part of Valentinian III's empire. Knowing he was unable to defeat the mighty Attila alone, the Western Roman Emperor forged an unlikely allegiance with his empire's former enemy: Theodoric I, king of the Visigoths, a western Europe tribe with Germanic roots. This new unified force faced off against Attila the Hun in the famous Battle of Catalaunian Plains (north-eastern France) in 451.

The Roman historian Jordanes documented Attila's bloodcurdling oration to his troops in his historical accounts. Jordanes was not a fan of Attila the Hun and may have only glamorised this speech because he knew of the outcome of the battle. Nevertheless, modern historians and rhetoricians are grateful for his account.

The structure of the speech roughly breaks down into four sections:

1. Attila compliments his audience for their past victories.
2. He insults the opposition.

3. He emboldens his troops to march for battle
4. He concludes with further compliments.

Stage One: Complimenting His Audience

There is an ancient rhetorical device called *comprobatio*. *Comprobatio* is when a speaker compliments an audience to further their own agenda: perhaps by building rapport or by empowering them to march into battle. In the opening of this speech, Attila used *comprobatio* for both of these purposes. Ironically, he opened his speech by telling his soldiers that they didn't need a speech. His words were:

> Here you stand, after conquering mighty nations and subduing the world. I therefore think it foolish for me to goad you with words, as though you were men who had not been proved in action. Let a new leader or an untried army resort to that. It is not right for me to say anything common, nor ought you to listen. For what is war but your usual custom? Or what is sweeter for a brave man than to seek revenge with his own hand? It is a right of nature to glut the soul with vengeance.

As with so many speeches before and after, Attila opened his oration by invoking the authority of time to emphasise the momentousness of what was happening. By speaking about the time or place that something is being said, a speaker grounds the audience in the moment. This is a rhetorical feature called *kairos*, the Greek word for time. From the opening words of 'Here you stand' to the reference of past conquests of 'after conquering mighty nations,' Attila was attempting to ground his troops in the moment.

It may seem strange to open a speech by saying 'Here you stand'. The audience surely would be aware that they were 'here' and know they were 'standing'. But by doing so, Attila used his opening to remind his listeners to be present in the moment. Indeed, from Attila the Hun to the Nazis, the rhetoric of 'here you stand' has been used time and time again to begin the process of hypnotising an audience. It has always been, and remains today, an effective way of grounding an audience before delivering a momentous message.

The objective of this part of the speech – especially 'after conquering mighty nations and subduing the world' – would have been intended to convince the soldiers that they were the best. Generally speaking, soldiers who believe that they are the best fight with more passion and determination than those who view themselves as ordinary or bedraggled, and, thus, are more likely to win. Attila may have believed his soldiers were the best, or he may have not, but he clearly knew that by stating that they were he would increase his chances of a swift and glorious victory. When we will look at Napoleon's addresses to his troops we will see the same flattery being delivered in the same way. If a dictator wants people to risk their lives or die in their name, they always start with flattery – often a combination of flattery and fear.

As part of this ritualistic flattery, Attila the Hun used *erotema* when he said, 'for what is war but your usual custom?' *Erotema* is a question for which no answer is needed. This is more commonly known as a rhetorical question. Not only do rhetorical questions engage an audience's attention by getting them to think, but statements in the form of questions often sound more genuine and sincere. *Erotema* can sometimes act to state the obvious but in a way that sounds philosophical.

Stage Two: Insulting the Enemy

After praising his troops, Attila went on to do what almost every wartime leader and football coach does: insult the enemy. In his own words:

> Let us then attack the foe eagerly; for they are ever the bolder who make the attack. Despise this union of discordant races! To defend oneself by alliance is proof of cowardice. See, even before our attack they are smitten with terror. They seek the heights, they seize the hills and, repenting too late, clamour for protection against battle in the open fields. You know how slight a matter the Roman attack is. While they are still gathering in order and forming in one line with locked shields, they are checked, I will not say by the first wound, but even by the dust of battle. Then on to the fray with stout hearts, as is your wont.

As he mocked and insulted the enemy, Attila the Hun used a rhetorical feature known as *argumentum ad hominem*. *Argumentum ad hominem* is when a speaker attacks the *ethos* of a person or group instead of making a more substantial point, such as, for example, challenging their logic. In this instance, Attila attempted to characterise his enemy as weak and feeble. Breaking it down, Attila accused the enemy of:

1. Forming a cowardly alliance out of fear of the Huns.
2. Seeking high ground and avoiding the open battlefield (also out of fear).
3. Being generally weak: he called their attacks 'slight' and suggested that they would fall not just from wounds but from the dust of battle itself.

Among his barrage of insults, Attila used a *tricolon* when he said: 'They seek the heights, they seize the hills and, repenting too late, clamour for protection against battle in the open fields.'

Technically, one might say that the great barbarian of popular imagination used a *tricolon of argumentum ad hominem* in the form of an *enthymeme*.

Stage Three: Riling up the Troops

After insulting the enemy, Attila went on to the most important part of any war speech, the call to violence:

> Despise their battle line. Attack the Alani[1], smite the Visigoths! Seek swift victory in that spot where the battle rages. For when the sinews are cut the limbs soon relax, nor can a body stand when you have taken away the bones. Let your courage rise and your own fury burst forth! Now show your cunning, Huns, now your deeds of arms! Let the wounded exact in return the death of his foe; let the unwounded revel in the slaughter of the enemy.

Attila could have said, 'go and kill the enemy', but that wouldn't have been as effective. By employing various rhetorical schemes and tropes, he managed to whip his soldiers into a blood-thirsty frenzy.

When Attila said, 'Attack the Alani, smite the Visigoths', he used a rhetorical feature known as *abundantia*. *Abundantia* is when a speaker uses multiple words which mean roughly the same thing. This form of repetition allows a speaker to emphasise a point: in

---

[1] The Alani were an Iranic people who also joined the Western Roman Empire in their campaign against Attila.

Attila the Hun's case, that they should kill the enemy. By employing two violent verbs instead of one ('attack' and 'smite'), Attila would have fired up the emotional charge felt by his fighters. Certain words hold more emotional meaning than others and such repetition melds these meanings together into one forceful climax. To add to this, if anyone in Attila's army had a particular hatred of either the Alani or the Visigoths, naming them would further fuel their lust for blood.

This extract shows us how Attila masterfully wielded *pathos* (use of emotion) to motivate his soldiers to unleash destruction. As well as displaying passion himself, he would have stirred passions in his listeners: passions of rage, courage, anger, vengeance. At one point, Attila said: 'Let your courage rise and your own fury burst forth!'

Using imperative sentences to command emotions is a powerful rhetorical tool which is often used to manipulate an audience into action (recall Mark Anthony's "Cry Havoc!' and let slip the dogs of war!' from the Introduction): this was exactly what Attila was attempting to do.

Taking a closer look at the extract of Attila's speech, one might notice that these last sentences are all commands: he instructed his soldiers how to feel and what to do. In the eyes of many, this is the language of true leadership.

As well as eliciting emotions, Attila used an abundance of imagery. From the boneless bodies to the slaughtered enemy, his words painted a picture of victory. When an audience is able to imagine something, they want it more. Some rhetoricians refer to the act of summoning vivid images in the audience's mind as *enargia*. Depicting a desirable result is a well-known tool of persuasion. Even today, centuries later, it is still used in marketing, war speeches and sales pitches.

The extract ends with *anaphora*. We can see this when Attila said: 'Let the wounded exact in return the death of his foe; let the unwounded revel in slaughter of the enemy.' These two clauses both start with 'Let the'. *Anaphora* is a form of repetition that makes a speech sound poetic and a statement sound exciting. Imagine if Winston Churchill just said, 'we shall fight them everywhere', as opposed to this more anaphorically dramatic version:

> We shall fight on the beaches, we shall fight on the landing grounds, we shall fight in the fields and in the streets, we shall fight in the hills; we shall never surrender.

Stage Four: More Compliments, the Supernatural, and Self-praise

After instructing his soldiers to march to battle, Attila the Hun continued to praise them by saying:

> No spear shall harm those who are sure to live; and those who are sure to die Fate overtakes even in peace. And finally, why should Fortune have made the Huns victorious over so many nations, unless it were to prepare them for the joy of this conflict. Who was it revealed to our sires the path through the Maeotian swamp[2], for so many ages a closed secret? Who, moreover, made armed men yield to you, when you were as yet unarmed? Even a mass of federated nations could not endure the sight of the Huns. I am not deceived in the issue; here is the field so many victories have promised us. I shall hurl the first

---

2 The Maeotian swamp is a geographical location in present-day Russia.

spear at the foe. If any can stand at rest while Attila fights, he is a dead man.

The last line is particularly interesting as Attila switched from praising 'us' to praising 'me'. In those final two sentences, Attila invoked his own *ethos*: 'if they face me, they die'. One might imagine that, in battle, having a leader who charges at the front rather than orders from the back is a motivational one – a leader one might feel emboldened to fight and die for.

As well as building up his own ethos to empower his troops in this fourth extract, Attila used emotive language and vivid imagery. By reminding them of their past victories, the two rhetorical questions in this final extract were probably designed to elicit pride and loyalty in his soldiers. Soldiers who believe they have fate and victory on their side fight better – as do soldiers who believe they are fighting on the side of *Flagellum Dei*, the Scourge of God.

Attila used a contrast when he referenced life and death, saying: 'No spear shall harm those who are sure to live; and those who are sure to die Fate overtakes even in peace'. The contrast of life and death is a powerful and emboldening trope which reminds an audience of the grander scheme of the universe – an existential concept that often empowers men to act. This use of contrast, similarly to the ones used by Caesar ('by her mother from the kings and on her father's side is akin to the immortal gods'), is a use of antithesis (an intentional contrast to create an effect on the audience).

The speech was a resounding success. Jordanes wrote: 'Inflamed by these words, [the soldiers] all dashed into battle.'

The End of Attila

Ironically, after this grand and motivating speech, the mighty Attila the Hun and his men lost. This was the first and – as far as records tell us – only time Attila lost a battle. Even in failure, Attila and his men managed to decimate most of the Western Roman armies and kill King Theodoric I.

Attila the Hun retreated, but he didn't spend long licking his wounds. He raised an even greater army than before and successfully invaded the Italian Peninsula once more in 452 AD. This time he prevailed, plundering cities and destroying everything in his path. He continued to do so until Pope Leo I convinced him to cease. Some accounts suggest that Attila the Hun's army was tired, diseased, and needed to turn back to avoid starvation; the Vatican's version of the story is that Pope Leo I scared the mighty Attila with visions of St Peter; others speculate that Attila was given a pile of money to turn back.

Around a year later, in 453 AD, Attila died, shortly after choosing a new wife. He didn't die on a battlefield, wielding a sword, or killing enemies; he died on his wedding night due to what Jordanes tells us was 'excessive joy'.

How does one bury a man like Attila? One diverts a river, buries Attila under the riverbed, releases the river to its original path, and then kills everyone who was involved in the burial. That is what happened and, to this very day, no one knows where Attila the Hun lies buried. Rumours suggest that he is buried in three layered coffins of gold, silver, and iron.

Even Attila the Hun, the mighty warrior, wielder of the sword of Mars, destroyer of kingdoms, gave eloquent speeches. They were manifestly not all blood and death; he spent a lot of effort complimenting his soldiers. This is because no tyrant, dictator or general can rule without people lower down supporting them: something we will look at more when we explore the speeches of another eastern warlord, the Mongol king Chinggis Khan.

Attila's oration is a good example of how speeches can be used to motivate people to fight battles. With the right combination of *pathos*, and appropriate *ethos* and all the accompaniments, Attila the Hun motivated his troops to make the ultimate sacrifice: to die for their leader.

Wu Zetian (624-705)
As depicted in an 18th-century album of portraits of 86 emperors of China. Originally published/produced in China, 18th century. (British Library, Shelfmark Or. 2231)

3.
WU ZETIAN

For more than 2,000 years, China was ruled by emperors. In all, there were 83 different dynasties and 559 emperors. Of these 559 emperors, only one was a woman. Although China's history was filled with influential women who ruled through their husbands and sons, Wu Zetian was the only one who became 'emperor' in her own right (in Mandarin she was referred to by the masculine noun). Her reign was known as the Wu Zhou Dynasty and lasted from 690-705 AD.

Reputedly through violence and deceit, Wu single-handedly disrupted the Tang dynasty: a dynasty which reigned both before and after her 15-year Zhou Dynasty.

How did Wu Zetian manage to break a Chinese dynasty? And what do we know of her speeches?

Wu's Rise to Power

Wu began her imperial life not as an empress but as a concubine. The emperors of China had many concubines (mistresses) as well as a hierarchy of wives, the most senior of whom was known as the

Empress Consort. The pre-pubescent Wu became a concubine to Emperor Taizong who, despite already having many women to keep him company, took an immediate liking to her.

Wu was documented – unverifiably – as using seductively violent words to impress the emperor and gain his favour. One of the stories recorded in the history books tells us of a time that Emperor Taizong had an unruly horse, Shizicong (Dappled Lion), who could not be tamed. Wu Zetian supposedly said to the emperor:

> I can tame him but will require three things: a metal whip, an iron rod, and a dagger. I will whip him, then if that does not work, I will strike his neck with the stick, and if that does not work, I will cut his throat with the dagger.

The two *tricolons* used in this extract are what are often referred to as 'ascending *tricolons*,' where each word is more powerful than the preceding one.

The first *tricolon* is a list of weapons each more menacing than the last: metal whip; iron rod; and dagger. In the second ascending *tricolon*, she explains what she will do: whip him; strike his neck; cut his throat – again, each step is more violent than the last.

There is also a new form of repetition here that we have not yet encountered. It is the repetition of 'if that does not work' which the young Wu repeated at the end of two successive clauses. Repeating something at the end of a clause, sentence or paragraph is known as *epistrophe*. *Epistrophe* is the rhetorical twin of *anaphora* (repetition at the beginning).

Wu had limited potential for progression with the ageing Emperor Taizong who was significantly older than her. His son and successor-apparent Gaozong, on the other hand, was a much more promising prospect. In his book *Wu*, the historian Jonathan Clements says that 'it is widely accepted that Wu and Gaozong were intimate before her 'husband' Taizong was dead'. It is worth noting that Gaozong was already married, had his own concubines, and was a few years younger than the then beautiful Wu who was, at this stage, a teenager.

After Taizong's death, Gaozong was made emperor and his chief wife became Empress Wang. Wu was then married to the new emperor, though with a lower status than his other concubines and wives.

To Emperor Gaozong's frustration, Empress Wang did not have any sons. To add to her woes, in 654, her emerging rival Wu gave birth to a girl who then mysteriously died. Wu blamed her daughter's death on Empress Wang, who was supposedly the last person to visit the newborn. Many myths speculate that, in order to raise her own rank with the emperor, Wu killed her own daughter to frame Empress Wang. Whatever the truth behind the infant's death, Wu is documented as having exploited it to demonise Empress Wang, who quickly fell out of grace with Emperor Gaozong. After some more unfortunate events, perhaps orchestrated by Wu (or perhaps not), Empress Wang was finally demoted, and Wu was given the position of chief wife, and consequently crowned Empress Wu.

As any tyrant will attest, once in the top spot you need to eliminate anyone who threatens your seat of power. Worried that the demoted former Empress Wang might one day rise again to be a threat, Wu had her killed. It was not a pleasant death. Some sources suggest that Wang's hands and feet were cut off and her mutilated body thrown into a vat of wine. This was a particularly horrible form of execution in which the victim usually took a few days to die. Wu is said to have visited Wang as she was drowning and made smug comments to the mutilated former empress.

Historians often believe that Wu was the driving influencer throughout Emperor Gaozong's reign until his death in 683. After Emperor Gaozong's death, Wu's son, Li Xian, became the next emperor. A few months after becoming emperor, his mother Wu was unhappy with his choices and wielded her influence in court to have her son deposed. He was banished and replaced by another of her sons, Li Dan. For the following years, Li Dan acted as a ceremonial figurehead while his mother continued to rule the empire, by telling him what to do. In 690, perhaps fed up with wielding power through other people, Wu had Li Dan deposed and banished, and took the throne herself. For the first and only time in Chinese history, a woman was officially emperor. Emperor Wu reigned until she too was deposed, by her two banished sons, Li Xian and Li Dan, who joined forces to oust her in a successful coup in 705.

Empress Wu was only able to become Emperor Wu through malice and deceit because the society in which she lived would have never otherwise allowed a woman to become Emperor. Because of this, Wu was vilified in contemporary and later sources; much of what was documented about her was done so from a biased male perspective.

The Vilification of Wu and Her Response

Unfortunately, the majority of the speeches and edicts that Wu gave are hidden in the various books of Chinese histories, such as the *Book of Tang*, which have never been translated into English in their entirety. Nevertheless, some academics have translated small sections of Chinese historical accounts which have allowed us to glimpse the rhetorical world in which Wu Zetian lived. The best example is an English translation of a speech about Wu.

During the rebellion led by the rebel general Li Jingye, a man named Lue Binwang gave a furious polemic that blasted Wu Zetian. Lue Binwang made outlandish accusations and attacked Wu's personality on every level. His objective was to sow anger and rage in his audience – fellow generals, soldiers, and civilians – so that they would turn against Emperor Wu and her reign. Here is a translation of the verbal attack (which Richard Guisso thankfully included in his book *Wu Tse-T'ien and other Politics of Legitimation in T'ang China*):

> The woman Wu, who has falsely usurped the throne, is by nature obdurate and unyielding, by origin, truly obscure. Formerly, she was among the lower ranks of the T'ai-tsung's servants and served him by changing his clothes. When she reached mature age, she brought disorder to the palace of the crown prince, concealing her private [relationship] with the former emperor.
>
> She then plotted covertly to gain favour in the Inner Chambers... and, concealing her mouth behind her sleeve, she skilfully slandered the other women. With cunning flattery and perverse artfulness, she deluded the ruler. She then usurped the regalia of empress and entrapped our ruler in incest.
>
> Then, with a heart like a serpent and a nature like a wolf, she favoured evil flatterers while destroying her good and loyal officials.
>
> She has killed her elder sister, butchered her elder brothers, murdered the ruler, poisoned her mother! She is hated by gods

and men alike; neither heaven nor earth can bear her. Still, she harbours calamitous intentions and plans [to steal] the sacred regalia [of the ruler]. The beloved son of the ruler she keeps in a separate palace, and she has given the most important offices [of state] to her own group of bandits.

In their attempts to sully the reputation of Wu Zetian, Lue Binwang made this polemic as scathing as possible. He would have done so in hope that it would persuade waverers to turn against Emperor Wu and join the rebellion; his objective was for people to take up arms and fight.

Unlike Attila the Hun, who targeted an enemy army, this character assassination is targeted against an individual and is a good example of *argumentum ad hominem*. Lue Binwang mentioned Wu's lowly rank, her sexual promiscuity, and her villainous deeds: all to corrupt her image. An important part of any tyrant's power is their image. And when other tyrants try to bring them down, their image is one of the first lines of attack.

By accusing her of cunning 'flattery and perverse artfulness', Lue Binwang targeted her ability to speak well. Throughout history, there has been a common movement against those who can speak convincingly, and it is interesting to see this brought as a criticism of Wu Zetian. Flattery is, as we know, a rhetorical trope itself (*comprobatio*) – so too is attacking someone for using it.

To further tarnish the *ethos* of Emperor Wu, the accuser used zoomorphic imagery. Zoomorphic imagery (presenting something or someone like an animal) is a common trait in the cannon of *ad hominem* rhetoric. The exact simile which Lue Binwang used was saying that Emperor Wu had a 'heart like a serpent and nature like a wolf'. The heart, being a very emotive organ on which life depends, is often invoked in comparisons to vilify – or glorify – people. Much character assassination tries to dehumanise a person or a group: usually as part of an argument which justifies treating them inhumanely.

Lue Binwang then went on to list people Wu has supposedly killed: 'She has killed her elder sister, butchered her elder brothers, murdered the ruler, poisoned her mother!' This *abundantia* serves the purpose of outraging the people. The words used ('killed', 'murdered', 'butchered', and 'poisoned') escalate in severity to climax with a concoction of unpleasant accusations, which ultimately mean 'she kills her own family members'.

The final feature worth highlighting from this extract is the use of *antithesis* which we can see when Lue Binwang said: 'She is hated by gods and men alike; neither heaven nor earth can bear her'. Contrasts are often used in this manner to emphasise the universality of something: in this case, that no one mortal or divine can tolerate Wu and her treachery. It is interesting to note that the contrast here links the supernatural and divine, as was done by Attila the Hun ('No spear shall harm those who are sure to live; and those who are sure to die Fate overtakes even in peace'); but also mentions the divine and the mortal, as was done by Julius Caesar ('by her mother from the kings and on her father's side is akin to the immortal gods'). If anything, this proves that certain elements of rhetoric transcend the location, era, or language in which they were used. There are some basic things that make us human, and they are found reflected in speeches across all cultures of history.

How did the great Emperor Wu Zetian react when she read a transcript of this personal and nasty attack on her character? Reportedly, she laughed out loud and said: 'Who is his speechwriter? A man that talented should be working for me!'

Seemingly unfazed by this rebellion and the words spoken against her, Wu Zetian crushed the rebellion. No tyrant worth mentioning will ever crush a rebellion without exploiting their victory afterwards. Rebellions are dangerous, but they are also an opportunity for publicity. In Wu's case, she wanted to issue a warning to everyone. After defeating the rebellion, she told her court:

> These three men were looked up to [with respect, but] they were harmful to me and I was able to destroy them. If [any of you] have abilities [which] surpass these three men, then you must act accordingly. If not, you should change your hearts and serve me, not making [yourselves an object of] ridicule for the empire.

In a textbook case of power play, Wu began by complimenting her opposition (they were 'looked up to with respect'). When the Romans destroyed Jerusalem in 70AD, they dismantled the city's walls, but they left the grandest tower in the ancient city's fortifications, the Phiasel Tower, standing to show the world how great the city's fortifications had been. In a similar fashion, Wu complimented the leaders of the rebellion to aggrandize the people she could overpower and destroy.

In many ways, this short oration is the ultimate tyrannical power play. A powerful leader says: 'These were great men. I killed them. Does anyone want to be next?' One can imagine that every man in that room was doing everything to avoid attracting Wu's attention.

While the primary translated sources available on Wu Zetian are sparse, it is clear to us that she, and her enemies, understood the role of rhetoric and speeches in propagating terror. Wu's enemies used rhetoric to rally troops against her; she used rhetoric to strike fear into the hearts of everyone around her. Perhaps she was a ruthless murderer who killed all of those people, or perhaps she wasn't. Either way, having people believe you are capable of such a thing is a step towards scaring them into submission. Fear, as we shall further explore, is a crucial weapon in the armoury of absolute power.

After Wu Zeitan was deposed in February 705, her life was spared by her sons who allowed her to live as Empress Regent. She died later the same year, the only female emperor in two millennia of Imperial China.

Chinggis Khan[a] (c. 1162-227).
Reproduction of a 1278 portrait paint and ink on silk taken from a Yuan-era album — National Palace Museum, Taipei.

4.
CHINGGIS KHAN

An Introduction to Temüjin

The dominant power structure of an era shapes how words are used to attain and wield power. In the late 12th and early 13th century Mongolia, power was distributed among chieftains, mighty men who would kill for fun, destroy entire tribes, and desecrate anything or anyone they didn't like. As you can imagine, these men, the pillagers and plunderers of 13th century Asia, didn't have Roman-style elections, an established democracy or citizens' assemblies. They had a super-macho mentality of kill, kill, kill.

Their leader was a man named Temüjin. Temüjin would later be given the honour of being renamed to Chinggis Khan (some people spell it 'Genghis' but I will use the less popular, but more correct, 'Chinggis').

Throughout his reign, Chinggis Khan is thought to be responsible for the deaths of approximately 40 million people. He rewarded his friends, and was ruthless to his enemies. He annihilated cities, wiped out populations, and eradicated empires. Despite Chinggis Khan's history of oppression, violence, and savagery, he is celebrated as a hero in modern-day Mongolia and his image appears on bank notes of the Mongolian Tugrik. Seven centuries since his death, his story is still embedded in culture, from novels to video games.

Yet contemporary sources are few and far between: 13th century Mongolia didn't have as scholarly an attitude to life as the Greeks and Romans and, as a result, a lot less was documented. The most valuable source we have on Chinggis Khan's life is *The Secret History of the Mongols*. This remarkable text is thought to have been written shortly after his death and glorifies his achievements. It records what he said to his friends, family, and the warlords in his court. From this single text, we can get a glimpse of how Chinggis was perceived by the anonymous author and what sort of rhetoric he supposedly used.

In the late 12th century, the Mongols were mostly nomadic. Famed for their horse skills, they travelled from place to place, living in yurts: round portable tents which were easy to move and provided relative luxury. When Temüjin was born in 1162, the Mongol empire did not exist and the power of the Mongols lay with clan leaders who managed their own tribes. They answered to the appointed Khan, but power wasn't particularly centralised.

Temüjin had a difficult upbringing. When he was still very young, his father, a clan leader, died, leaving him in a state of penury. Despite this, as he grew into adulthood, Temüjin gained followers and status and rose through the ranks of the Mongolian ruling class.

At one point in his youth, his camp was raided by an enemy tribe known as the Merkits. Temüjin was captured in his youth and (like Caesar) held hostage. His wife, Börte, was also captured at the same time. After some ritual humiliation from his captors, the young Temüjin managed to escape.

Fleeing the Merkits, Temüjin went to his powerful friends – warlords and chieftains – his sworn brothers, and told them that his wife was hostage to the Merkits. At a gathering, each of his friends pledged to give him some form of military support with an accompanying ceremonial speech. A man named Jamuqa, one of Temüjin's sworn brothers, lavishly declared his allegiance by saying:

> I have made offerings
>
> to the long spear-tipped banner,
>
> I have beaten the cow-hide drum
>
> that sounds with a deep rumble,
>
> I have ridden my swift grey [horse],
>
> I have put on my leather-thonged armour,
>
> I have grasped my hilted sword,
>
> I have set my notched arrow [against the string],
>
> Let us battle to the death against the Uduyit-Merkits

While this is not Chinggis himself speaking, it gives a flavour of Mongol rhetoric from the ruling class in the 12th century. From the *anaphoric* repetition of past tense 'I have' to the contrasting future plural imperative of 'Let us', the rhetoric in this extract is muscular and, above all, rhythmic. This structural repetition – using clauses of similar lengths – is synonymous with many war speeches, which often follow a rhythmic 'thump'. Using clauses or sentences of a similar length to create a rhythm is a rhetorical feature known as an *isocolon*.

As with many war speeches, Jamuqa's declaration of allegiance ended with an imperative to 'battle to the death': an absolute claim of determination to the end. What is the driving rhetoric behind invoking death? It is that of time and determination: one could classify it as both *kairos* (use of time) and *pathos* (use of emotion). Similarly to Attila the Hun and Jamuqa, many leaders invoke the seriousness of death in speeches to motivate soldiers or state the seriousness of a matter.

Another role that this rhetoric played within that power structure, was to excite the anticipation of the other warlords who were listening in the meeting, each of whom said something different in support of the young Temüjin and his wife.

In contrast to Jamuqa's rather poetic declaration, To'otil Qan, said:

I will crush the Merkits

and rescue Lady Börte for you.

In return for the black sable jacket,

I will break all the Merkits into pieces and bring back your qatan Börte.

In many ways, it seems like To'otil Qan just repeated the same thing twice without much variation. It is possible that in the original language this repetition would have been a form of *abundantia*, but it is also possible that he was just a clumsy speaker.

What happened next? Temüjin, Jamuqa, To'otil Qan, and his other warlord friends unleashed the full Mongol hell on the Merkits. The Mongol victory was so overwhelming, that the history books recorded how the Merkits were 'crushed and blown away like ashes'. Temüjin was reunited with his wife, and became famous for having secured such a great victory. Thus began Temüjin's journey to building the world's mightiest empire.

As it happens, Temüjin's good 'friend' Jamuqa became an obstacle to his rise from power and their friendship deteriorated into a rivalry that ended in a war, which Jamuqa lost. Jamuqa was executed, as were a number of other rivals, and Temüjin ruled the Mongols with undisputed authority. In 1206, after having vanquished all serious opposition, he adopted the name Chinggis Khan (which loosely translates to 'universal leader').

To truly make himself the most feared man in the world, Chinggis Khan had to follow the steps of Attila the Hun and overpower the biggest empire in the region. For Attila the Hun, it was the two Roman empires; for Chinggis Khan, it was China. China had changed a lot since the death of Wu Zeitan and the end of the Tang dynasty, but it was still one of the greatest powers in the world.

In 1209, Chinggis invaded the Western Xia Empire, which eventually submitted to his rule. The following year, he launched an invasion against the mighty Jin dynasty. By 1215, he had already managed to capture the capital city of Zhongdu (now called Beijing). Under Chinggis Khan's rule, the Mongols pillaged most of the North China plain.

All the way from Korea to Europe, covering nearly 18% of the world's land, Chinggis Khan formed the largest empire the world had ever seen. It dwarfed the empires of the Romans, the Huns and the entire Tang dynasty. (To this day, only one empire ever managed to best it: the British Empire, which occupied 26.3% of the globe).

The Rhetoric of Chinggis Khan

Unlike Jordanes' account of Attila the Hun's dramatic battle speech, the speeches we have for Chinggis Khan were not delivered to troops, but to his close friends and confidants. Chinggis Khan would have councils that he would address, and we have those addresses. In them, he praised his allies, mocked his enemies and gave out orders and commands. One such command went as follows:

> Slice through the necks of the strong.
> Empty the breasts of the arrogant.

While this wasn't uttered on the battlefield, it carries a similar sentiment to Attila's war speech where he ordered his troops to, 'Attack the Alani, smite the Visigoths' and spoke of broken bodies such as 'when the sinews are cut the limbs soon relax, nor can a body stand when you have taken away the bones'. Chinggis Khan used evocative imagery for a violent call to action. This quote is a good sample of the poetic language attributed to Chinggis Khan in *The Secret History of the Mongols*.

Structurally, both sentences follow a similar pattern:

1. A violent verb
2. A name of a body part (one that is essential to life)
3. An adjective to describe the enemy

By repeating these three points in both of his sentences, Chinggis Khan infused the message behind his words with an almost poetic passion. Such structural repetition is a way of emphasising a point and making sure that everyone understands the assignment. Metaphors, imagery, and emotive references to empower orders are commonly found in the documented words of most tyrants before and after Chinggis Khan.

The Secret History of the Mongols shares many examples of Chinggis Khan ordering the deaths of his enemies. Like other leaders, Chinggis Khan uses character assassination to discredit the people he is speaking about before sentencing them to death. A good example of this is when he gave the following order to the great council after defeating the Tartars in battle:

> From early days the Tartars have destroyed our ancestors and fathers. [We must] gain vengeance on behalf of our fathers, we must seek revenge for our ancestors. Let them be killed. We will measure them against a linchpin and kill off [those who are taller than the linchpin] until all have died. We will make slaves of the survivors.

Chinggis Khan makes a point of emphasising the villainy of the Tartars before ordering their execution. Despite this being a particularly bloody order, he used emotive language, invoking the memory of the fallen when he spoke of 'vengeance on behalf of our fathers' and 'revenge for our ancestors'. Such *pathos* would have been intended to elicit anger from his fellow Mongols, who would have suffered grief. This anger, which he summoned to his audience, was then satisfied with the simple order: 'Let them be killed'. Many tyrants make a point of performatively giving people what they want, and Chinggis Khan did in this extract.

The reason that Chinggis Khan made a performance out of this death sentence is that it would have made his listeners like him more, fear him more, and see him as the powerful leader they all wanted. Ultimately, this performance was not about the execution, it was about Chinggis Khan using the execution as an opportunity to build his reputation and consolidate his power. As we've already learnt, dictators and tyrants seize any opportunity to speak in front of influential people.

Pathos in Praise

It might come as a surprise that this mighty warrior, slayer of kings, and destroyer of empires gave warm-hearted speeches, but he did – for a good reason.

Chinggis Khan relied on support from the other Mongol chieftains, who he strategically rewarded and kept on side. One of the ways he would do so was through flattery. While Attila the Hun used *comprobatio* to bolster his soldiers' resolve in the face of a mighty battle, Chinggis Khan flattered individuals in the relative calm of his council. Whatever the context, flattery often goes hand in hand with some meaningful and emotional language.

When praising and thanking his fellow chieftains, Chinggis Khan often deployed *pathos* to shower them with friendship and glory. While praising people, he would often provide accompanying anecdotes to demonstrate his sincerity. When Chinggis Khan publicly praised Father Munglig, a close friend with whom he grew up, he said:

> You, my old and good friend,
>
> you who were born at the same time I was born
>
> and who has grown up together with me,
>
> how many times have you served and protected me?
>
> I remember one time when my father Ong Khan and Anda Senggum, plotting against me,

called me to their camp,

and on the way I passed the night in the tent of Father Munglig.

If you hadn't convinced me to turn back

I would have been drowned in the whirlpool,

I would have been consumed by the fire.

With that service in mind

how could I ever forget you?

With that service in mind

I'll have you sit on a seat at the corner of my throne

and I'll ask you the meaning of the month and the year.

I'll give you favours and gifts

and I will serve you for generations to come.

By invoking their youth like he would for siblings, Chinggis Khan emphasised his close relation to Munglig, almost alluding to them being like brothers. This use of emotive language, whether spontaneous or pre-scripted, would have been designed to elicit a response from Munglig as well as the wider council who were also listening.

Chinggis Khan clearly understood the power of stories to connect with an audience, as almost all of his praise comes in the form of flattering stories about the person he is addressing. All speakers, tyrants or otherwise, know that a story will usually elicit a stronger response than a statistic or philosophical musing.

To further emphasise how grateful he was for Munglig's support, Chinggis Khan used a wild exaggeration to emphasise his point (a rhetorical trick known as *hyperbole*). We can see this when he said:

'I would have been drowned in the whirlpool, // I would have been consumed by the fire.' The contrasting imagery of fire and water – an *antithesis of enargeia* (vividness) – is a common motif found throughout almost all cultures. His gratefulness was further emphasised by the anaphoric repetition ('I would' and 'I'll') in the speech.

At the beginning of the extract, Chinggis Khan spoke of the past and he ended by speaking about the future, both with warmth. The reference to the past created a bond between him and his audience, and the promise for the future helped ensure that loyalty for that bond remained ironclad. This structural *antithesis* would have again given the impression of sincerity. Using positive imagery of hope is an important part of keeping supporters in line. It reminds them of the value they are fighting for. In some cases, it makes them believe they are fighting for a value rather than a tyrant.

Before continuing, we need to consider why Chinggis Khan praised Munglig in this way in front of an audience? It is important to note that he didn't just do this for Munglig: Munglig was just one of many generals who received his praise during that particular speech. The reason that the great Khan did this was to consolidate the loyalty of his supporters. When people see someone being showered with glory, they usually want to work harder to achieve similar glory. As a further incentive, Chinggis Khan, in these speeches, would often give – or make promises to give – things to his faithful men: he promised his loyal chieftains land, troops, and even the wives of other men. On one occasion, he even gifted someone one of his own wives as a reward for their support.

In another part of the same speech, Chinggis Khan praised Khubilai, Jelme, Jebe, and Subetei:

> You've pressed at the necks of mighty soldiers in my service,
>
> you've brought down the mounts of strong men.
>
> When I sent for my four dogs,
>
> my Khubilai, Jelme, Jebe, and Subetei,
>
> ordering you to go out against what I saw before me,
>
> you were there shattering the stones when I said, 'Go there!'
>
> You rode out smashing the cliffs the moment I said, 'Attack!'
>
> breaking the brightest gems into pieces
>
> and cutting the deep waters in two.

In contrast to the praise of Munglig, this doesn't evoke a sense of family pathos but a sense of power: a *pathos* of pride. Once more, Chinggis Khan framed his praise in the form of a story, and once more, he used hyperbolic metaphors to emphasise the greatness of the people he was addressing. Natural imagery and the force of nature are popular themes in poetry and rhetoric. We can see them used here when Chinggis Khan suggests that they smashed cliffs and cut deep water into two.

As much praise as Chinggis Khan had for other people, in true dictatorial style he reserved the highest praise for himself. While he praised and exaggerated the feats of his supporters, when speaking of himself, he would often use language with undertones of divinity. For example:

> Now thanks to Eternal Blue Heaven
>
> My power has been increased by Heaven and Earth.
>
> I've straightened out the lives of the entire Nation
>
> and they're controlled by the reins in my hands.

Chinggis Khan attributed his success to a higher order (the Eternal blue Heaven refers to the divine) and then, through the metaphor of holding the reins, bluntly declared: 'I am in control and I have all the power'. The contrast of Heaven and Earth is another common pairing which is used almost universally when making grand statements. While this was used in a positive sense, it is exactly the same as the *antithesis* used by the rebel Lue Binwang against Wu Zetian.

Chinggis Khan was aware that some might try to cross him so he ended one of his edicts with a direct warning:

> Any person who does not obey this order will be punished.
>
> Any person who's accepted to serve in my presence and doesn't serve properly,
>
> I'll send such a man out of my sight and exile him to a distant land.

Moving along from *comprobatio* and *pathos*, it is interesting to see moments where Chinggis Khan was almost egalitarian when it came to recruiting soldiers. On one occasion, he said:

> Let the ablest and best-looking men step forward,
>
> the sons of captains of ten thousand,
>
> of thousands, of hundreds, of tens,
>
> and the sons of common soldiers,
>
> any man who is worthy to serve in my presence.

By listing all the different numbers, Chinggis Khan used *abundantia* (listing many words with a similar meaning). He could have said: 'Everyone is welcome to apply'. But by saying 'the sons of captains of ten thousand, // of thousands, of hundreds, of tens, // and the sons of common soldiers' Chinggis Khan emphasised that truly everyone was welcome to join.

No matter their rank, status, or the number of men controlled by their fathers, the men listening to this speech would have felt personally addressed. Speeches are always strongest when members of the audience feel a personal connection to the speaker. That is why speakers use *pathos* to tailor their address to specific groups or communities.

The End of Chinggis Khan

In August 1227, in his mid-sixties, Chinggis Khan died. People don't fully know how or why he died; some historians suggest it could have been related to an injury from falling off of a horse. What we do know is that he died during a campaign to quash a rebellion in the kingdom of Xi Xia. Before he died, on his deathbed, he ordered that Xi Xia be wiped off the face of the earth. As per his instructions, the kingdom of Xi Xia was obliterated, in what some scholars claim is the first documented genocide. Entire cities and towns were annihilated and all of their inhabitants killed or enslaved.

Even in death, his words remade the world.

*Isabella I of Castile (1451-1504).
Anonymous portrait of Isabella I, c. 1490.*

5.
THE QUEENS OF EUROPE

While Wu Zetian battled her way to the top position, other women were born into power. It is easy for us, in an era of postmodern feminism, to look back on historical queens as gender champions battling against a male-dominated world of injustice. Many probably were, but they were also tyrants and murderers. They ruled with iron fists, they were responsible for committing atrocities, and they gave speeches which consolidated power, instilled fear, and championed bloody death in battle.

There were three particularly significant tyrannical queens in Europe in under 200 years: the Spanish Queen Isabella I of Castile and the English sisters Queen Mary I and Queen Elizabeth I.

Isabella I of Castile

Isabella of Castile is sometimes championed as the first major female European monarch to hold power independent from a male chaperone. She wielded her power like so many of the power-drunk tyrants who came before her, by abusing her people.

Two of the most barbaric acts of abuse from Isabella of Castile were the Spanish Inquisition and the expulsion of the Jews from Spain. The Spanish Inquisition was a legal and religious body set up to root out Jews who had converted to Catholicism but who had secretly kept some of their Jewish identity or traditions. Most of these people converted to Catholicism reluctantly because they were forced to do so through social and economic pressure. Such pressure often included threats, violence, and intimidation. Many of these reluctant converts secretly kept some of their Jewish traditions, and that did not sit well with the Spanish Catholics. These converts who secretly held on to part of their past identity were known as *marranos* (a Spanish word that translates to pigs or dirty person).

In its quest to uphold the Christian faith, the barbaric Spanish Inquisition was granted permission to do whatever it wanted to the Catholic converts. Largely, this meant torturing the peaceful Jewish-turned-Catholic population of Spain until they either convinced their torturer that they were truly Catholic or died. As people were being tortured, they ended up confessing to crimes of faith that they hadn't actually committed. These 'crimes of faith' include things like fasting on Yom Kippur or not working on the Sabbath, both of which are important customs in the Jewish faith. Once they confessed, they had to face the appropriate punishment. The torture was not just used for men, but also on women and children.

While the *marranos* were being persecuted, the (unconverted) Jewish population of Spain continued to live as third-class citizens in a society which systematically excluded and oppressed them. However, after a series of viciously calculated and wholly false claims that Jews were murdering children to use their blood for sacrilegious rituals, the Grand Inquisitor, Tomás de Torquemada, convinced Queen

Isabella to banish the Jews entirely. After their expulsion in 1492, approximately 40,000 to 150,000 Spanish Jews were forced to flee the country, leaving behind the lives they had built for themselves.

Queen Isabella was a strong woman in a world dominated by men and it is understandable that some people who are not so versed in her history would want to glorify her. Nevertheless, she was still a despot. And, just like the rest of them, she used rhetoric to get her way.

Isabella's Speeches

In 1476, during the Portuguese War, what threatened to be a serious rebellion broke out in Segovia, a city in Castile. Isabella decided to ride to the city and address the trouble head on. When she arrived at the gates of Segovia, guards urged her not to enter as the insurgents could be dangerous. While some leaders would have retreated in fear at the thought of facing an angry rabble, Queen Isabella I proclaimed:

> Tell these knights and citizens of Segovia that I am Queen of Castile, and that this city is mine... I need not laws or conditions, such as they would impose, to enter into my own.

This was an expression of *ethos*. Not only was Isabella asserting her own dominance, she was also reminding everyone around her that their place was to obey: not to impose conditions for her to follow. She wielded, demonstrated, and consolidated her power – all in the same sentence.

As the gates were reluctantly opened at the Queen's command, the angry mob ran through them and called for the death of the Marquis. The Marquis was the man responsible for their anger and subsequent rebellion.

To calm the people, Isabella reportedly said:

> My vassals, what do you seek? For that which is your good is my service, and I am pleased that it should be done.

Isabella made a point of addressing the people directly. By doing so, she not only added a sense of formality, she also reinforced the need for them to listen. Stating who you are talking to in this way is known as direct address and is an important part of any speech (not just the tyrannical type).

Isabella also aligned her values with the audience's through her emotive words. She spoke of her own values to convince the rebels that she genuinely cared about their demands. By doing so, she managed to placate them and the rebellion was over. As for the Marquis who caused them the initial offence, she just put him back in the same role. There was no second rebellion.

In essence, this story shows us how tyrants are able to use rhetoric to deceive an audience. The people were made to feel seen, and then nothing was done about their grievance. Leaders often know too well how the passions of rebellion can be short-lived, and placating the passion temporarily can kill off the entire movement. Placating a movement or passion with the tranquilising drug of gradualism is often easier than just giving the people what they originally wanted.

Similarly to how Chinggis Khan flattered the people who were crucial for propping up his regime, so too did Isabella. A good example of this can be seen in this letter she sent to Christopher Columbus:

> It is very good [to have] a learned man who has much experience of the matters of the sea. I am grateful to you and hold it a special obligation and service, both for your timeliness in sending it (as your warning and advice was most useful to us), as for having tendered it with the true goodwill and affection which have

always been known to you; and so believe that all is received as coming from a special and faithful servant of mine.

Every leader knows that if the people feel loved, they serve you better. The trick is knowing which people need to feel the love, and which people need to feel the fear. Once you identify the appropriate emotion, you apply the appropriate rhetoric. With her knights in the Rebellion of Segovia, Isabella wanted to invoke fear to get her way. In her letter to Columbus, she used flattery to secure his dedication. All messages need to have a clearly defined purpose – an objective that you want to achieve – and the rhetoric framing that purpose has to be suitably chosen. It is clear from these two examples that Isabella I knew exactly what she wanted, and how to get it.

In 1504, at the age of 53, Isabella I died of what is believed to be natural causes. Due to the positive contribution that she made to Christian life during her reign, many people want her to be made a saint. The official process of canonization has been discussed since the 1950s and is still ongoing today within the Catholic community. Her mistreatment of Jews in her kingdom is used as an argument against this.

Mary I (1516-558).
Portrait by Antonis Mor, 1554 in The Yorck Project (2002).

Mary I

Twelve years after the death of Queen Isabella I of Castile, her granddaughter was born. The child was the daughter of King Henry VIII of England and his first wife Catherine of Aragon, the daughter of Isabella I.

History often bestows significant characters with nicknames such as Alexander the Great or Suleiman the Magnificent. This granddaughter of Isabella would be remembered as Bloody Mary, also known as Queen Mary I of England.

Queen Mary's father Henry VIII famously had six wives. His first wife was Catherine of Aragon, whom he divorced because she failed to give him a son. His second was Anne Boleyn, whom he had beheaded for high treason. His third wife was Jane Seymour, who died during the birth of his son Edward. His fourth wife was Anne of Cleves, whom he divorced because he thought she was unattractive. His fifth wife was Catherine Howard, whom he had beheaded for adultery. His final wife was Katherine Parr, who outlived him.

Henry VIII attempted to petition the Pope for an annulment from Mary's mother by claiming that she consummated her first marriage. Before marrying Henry VIII, Catherine of Aragon was married to his older brother, Arthur, who died before becoming king. Under usual circumstances, the Pope might have listened; however, Rome had just been sacked by the soldiers of the Spanish King Carlos V, who now had the Pope at his mercy. As it happened, Carlos V was the grandchild of Isabella of Castile, which meant that Catherine of Aragon, the woman whom Henry VIII was attempting to divorce and disgrace, was his aunt. The Pope at the time wasn't inclined to offer an annulment to the husband of his captor's aunt. Outraged that an annulment was not granted, Henry VIII broke from Rome, left the Catholic Church, and turned to Protestantism.

Little Mary, who was still a child at the time, had a Catholic mother with phenomenally powerful relatives, and an angry Protestant father who accused her mother of marrying him under false pretences. Mary, herself a Catholic, became Queen of England in 1553, following the death of her sickly brother Edward VI.

It is estimated that she had over 300 people burnt during her five-year reign. This included some leading Protestants such as Thomas Cranmer, the Archbishop of Canterbury. In an attempt to save his life, Cranmer converted back to Catholicism and confessed his sins as a Protestant. Mary, wanting to make an example of him, had him burned at the stake anyway.

John Foxe, in his famous *Book of Martyrs*, remarked of Mary: 'Having obtained the sword of authority, she was not sparing in its exercise'.

Transitioning a country from Protestantism back to Catholicism in such a short period of time caused significant turmoil. Especially as the royal family was religiously split. Mary married the Catholic King of Spain Philip II, the son of Carlos V, grandchild of Isabella I, and thus Mary's first cousin. Through Mary's own faith, and now this ultra-Catholic union, Catholicism had a strong hold on England. Despite this, the English Protestant movement had hope.

Queen Mary had a Protestant half-sister, Princess Elizabeth, who was the daughter of Anne Boleyn (Henry VIII's second wife, whom he executed). A number of influential Protestants who managed to stay alive, wanted to see Princess Elizabeth on the throne of England. This led to a rebellion known as the Wyatt Rebellion. The rebellion sought to overthrow Mary and replace her with her Protestant half-sister, returning the kingdom to Protestantism.

The Wyatt Rebellion was the cause for Mary's most famous oration, which became known as the Guildhall Speech.

The Guildhall Speech

Unlike her grandmother Isabella I who faced a disgruntled rabble, Mary I found herself facing a fully-armed and organised rebellion, which she could not defeat with words alone. Any 16th century ruler would have been able to tell you that when words don't work, you send in the swords. However, those swords can be sharpened by the words of their master.

Talking to her troops before battling to quash the Wyatt Rebellion, Mary used her rhetorical skills to motivate them to fight for her cause. When you want people to die for you, the best way is to convince them that you like them and then give them as much confidence as possible. Rhetorically, that means *comprobatio* and *ethos*. Mary I gave a speech in which she used flattery and the establishment of her own character, just as Attila the Hun did. Here are some words taken from the opening of Mary's speech:

> Now, loving subjects, what I am ye right well know. I am your Queen, to whom at my coronation, when I was wedded to the realm and laws of the same (the spousal ring whereof I have on my finger, which never hitherto was, not hereafter shall be, left off), you promised your allegiance and obedience to me. And that I am the right and true inheritor of the Crown of this Realm of England, I take all Christendom to witness.

It is hard not to notice the striking resemblance to her grandmother Isabella's speech to the guards in the Segovia Rebellion. Both assert their *ethos* as 'The Queen' and remind the audience of their duty and allegiance to serve the monarch.

In contrast to Attila the Hun, Mary did not have a strong military background to motivate her troops, so she took a different approach to her assertion of leadership. She did, however, begin with flattery. She did this through the use of the adjective 'loving'. It may not seem like much, but this tiny adjective was an acknowledgement of their loyalty, the same loyalty she was depending on in that moment to defeat the enemy.

After the polite direct address which made a point of highlighting their loyalty, Mary then went on to further establish her credibility as their leader. She stated that she was married to the nation and that since her coronation, she hadn't removed her ring, which she referred to as 'spousal'. Her reason for saying this is that some people questioned her loyalty to the country. By marrying King Philip II of Spain, some felt that she had undermined her responsibility to England. By emphasising that she was the Queen of England and that she was wearing the ring of the monarch, she was reminding everyone of her steadfast loyalty to her country.

To further emphasise this, Mary used what is sometimes referred to as genetic fallacy. The genetic fallacy is where you argue that something is true based on where it comes from. In this instance, she invoked the authority of her late father, King Henry VIII:

> My Father, as you all know, possessed the same regal state, which now rightly is descended unto me; and to him always you showed yourselves most faithful and loving subjects, and

therefore I doubt not, but you will show yourselves likewise to me [...]

Reminding her listeners of her father's 'regal state' through this form of genetic fallacy is a use of both *logos* and *ethos*. If you map out what she said as a logical syllogism, it may look something like this:

Minor premise 1: You gave my father loyalty and obedience.
Minor premise 2: I have the same status as my father.
Conclusion: Therefore, I deserve the same loyalty and obedience.

After invoking the authority of her father, she then employed that age-old trick of insulting the enemy (*argumentum ad hominem*). Of Thomas Wyatt and his rebellion, she said:

> [...] therefore I doubt not, but you will show yourselves likewise to me, and that you will not suffer a vile traitor to have the order and governance of our person, and to occupy our estate, especially being so vile a traitor as Wyatt is. Who most certainly as he hath abused my ignorant subjects, which be on his side, so doth he intend and purpose the destruction of you, and spoil of your goods.

Generally speaking, when vilifying people, a tyrant or dictator will use whatever the people love most, and then say that the enemy is threatening that: if the people love wealth and money, then the enemy is threatening their wealth and money; if the people love peace and freedom, then the enemy is threatening their peace and freedom; if the people love democracy, then the enemy is threatening their democracy. In this case, Mary accused Wyatt of wanting to 'destroy' the audience and 'spoil' their goods.

Mary then finished her speech with the traditional battle cry ending which we've already looked at with other tyrants. Her words were:

> And now, good subjects, pluck up your hearts, and, like true men, stand fast against these rebels, both our enemies and yours, and fear them not; for I assure you I fear them nothing at all. And I will leave with you my Lord Howard, and my lord-treasurer, who shall be assistance with the mayor of your defence.

Similarly to tyrants before her, Bloody Mary used *kairos* before a battle to invoke a sense of urgency when she opened her sentence with 'And now'. Similarly to how *kairos* would have had an emboldening effect on Attila the Hun's troops, so, too, would it have been for Mary's.

Mary I's troops defeated Thomas Wyatt and quashed his rebellion. Sir Thomas Wyatt was hung, drawn and quartered, and his co-conspirators sentenced to similarly grisly deaths. After the rebellion, Bloody Mary locked her half-sister, Princess Elizabeth, in the Tower of London: a grand dungeon of torture where a number of royals had been imprisoned over the years.

*Elizabeth I (1533-1603).
The Darnley Portrait, c.1575, was named after a previous
owner. The author of the painting is unknown.*

Elizabeth I

Not long after imprisoning Princess Elizabeth in the Tower of London, Bloody Mary died, probably of cancer. As Mary I had no children, the line of succession looped back round to Elizabeth, who became Queen Elizabeth I.

Elizabeth wasn't as tyrannical as Isabella or Mary, and certainly not like her father Henry VIII. However, she was understandably ruthless. Elizabeth placed her Catholic cousin, Mary Queen of Scots, under house arrest and, after having found out that she posed a threat to the crown of England, had her executed. No matter how glorified Elizabeth I may be in the history books, executing your family relation in case they pose a threat to your power is tyrannical behaviour.

On Elizabeth's orders, English pirates plundered Spanish ships returning with treasures from the Americas. Much of that stolen treasure was given to Elizabeth who then allowed, and perhaps encouraged, them to continue their seafaring robbery. The King of Spain, still Philip II, was not happy about this. He was particularly insulted because, a few decades prior to all the piracy, after the death of his wife Bloody Mary, he proposed to Elizabeth I: a proposal she swiftly rejected.

Having been romantically rejected, and now publicly robbed, the King of Spain decided to launch his most powerful force against England: the Spanish Armada. This invasion is the context for the speech that Elizabeth gave to her troops at Tilbury, a port near London, in 1588. It is arguably the most famous speech ever delivered by an English monarch.

The Tilbury Speech

Faced with the prospect of annihilation by the mightier Spanish troops, the 55-year-old Queen Elizabeth, adorned in battle armour, rode her white horse onto a field at Tilbury to speak to her soldiers. There are several accounts of what she said. Here is the most famous:

> My loving people,
>
> We have been persuaded by some that are careful of our safety, to take heed how we commit ourselves to armed multitudes, for fear of treachery; but I assure you I do not desire to live to distrust my faithful and loving people. Let tyrants fear.
>
> I have always so behaved myself that, under God, I have placed my chiefest strength and safeguard in the loyal hearts and good-will of my subjects; and therefore I am come amongst you, as you see, at this time, not for my recreation and disport, but being resolved, in the midst and heat of the battle, to live and die amongst you all; to lay down for my God, and for my kingdom, and my people, my honour and my blood, even in the dust.

In this opening extract, Elizabeth directly addresses her 'loving people' in the same way Mary did, to the same effect. Instead of talking about the rings on her finger and her right to rule through her family history, Elizabeth directly spoke about fear. This emotive language would have been designed to address how the audience was feeling and turn it around. Elizabeth did so with her use of *antithesis* when she said: 'Let tyrants fear'. In saying this, she told her audience that they were the cause of fear in the Spanish troops – an emboldening thought. (Both Mary and Elizabeth spoke about fear in their respective war speeches as a way of countering their audience's natural emotional state before battle. This links back to that core message of knowing your audience).

Elizabeth then used *antithesis* again when she said that she was 'resolved, in the midst and heat of the battle, to live and die amongst you all'. The emotive contrast of 'live and die' is exactly the same as the one used by Attila the Hun. It is a common emotive contrast that has been used throughout the ages to distort an audience's perception of danger. In saying all of this, Elizabeth I also demonstrated her character and created a desirable *ethos*.

This opening extract ends with a very powerful *tricolon*, the rule of three. The queen declared that she was willing to die for 'my God, and for my kingdom, and my people'. In essence, this is a reverse ascending *tricolon*. Instead of starting with the least significant and building up, she does the reverse. Elizabeth's words might suggest that her biggest priority, above religion, and nation, was her people. This would have been particularly unifying, given England's turbulent history of switching twice from Catholic to Protestant in two decades.

After this dramatic opening, Elizabeth further consolidated her position by addressing the biggest concern that her 16th century audience had: that they were being led by a woman. She said:

> I know I have the body of a weak and feeble woman; but I have the heart and stomach of a king, and of a king of England too, and think foul scorn that Parma or Spain, or any prince of Europe, should dare to invade the borders of my realm: to which rather than any dishonour shall grow by me, I myself will take up arms, I myself will be your general, judge, and rewarder of every one of your virtues in the field.

Addressing the issue of gender head on, Elizabeth I deployed yet another use of *antithesis* to show her *ethos* not as a woman but as a monarch (for which, it is worth noting, she used the masculine 'king'). She then used *anaphora* (repetition at the start of speech) when she repeated 'I myself will'. This statement further supported her claim that she would be active in this conflict. The second use of 'I myself will' then led up to the *tricolon* of her being their 'general, judge, and rewarder'. Through her words, Elizabeth I made clear to her troops, not only that she was in charge, but that she deserved to be followed.

She then closed her address by saying:

> I know already, for your forwardness you have deserved rewards and crowns; and we do assure you in the word of a prince, they shall be duly paid you. In the meantime, my lieutenant general shall be in my stead, than whom never prince commanded a more noble or worthy subject; not doubting but by your obedience to my general, by your concord in the camp, and your valour in the field, we shall shortly have a famous victory over those enemies of my God, of my kingdom, and of my people.

Again, we can see the repetition of the reversed ascending *tricolon* 'of my God, of my kingdom, and of my people'.

Interestingly, Elizabeth did not give a battle cry in the form of an imperative as so many others before her did. Instead, she spoke of values, virtues, and rewards. Perhaps this is a distinction between the true tyrants of the world, and the nobler leaders.

Elizabeth I was victorious, and the Spanish Armada was defeated, because of strategic errors on the part of the Spanish and vicious storms which wrecked Spanish ships. Queen Elizabeth I had managed to secure her sovereignty and ward off one of the mightiest aggressors that the island nation had ever seen.

Her rule was relatively peaceful. She showed more religious tolerance than her sister. When she died of old age in 1603, the crown of England went to King James VI of Scotland. James VI was the son of Mary Queen of Scots, the Catholic queen beheaded by Elizabeth I.

*Napoleon Bonaparte (1769-1821).
The Emperor Napoleon crossing the Alps, 1800
by Jacques-Louis David.*

6.
NAPOLEON BONAPARTE

Despite coming from lower nobility, not actually being French, and having a short temper, Napoleon Bonaparte managed to become Emperor of France and the most powerful man in the world. Not only did he elevate his own position but also that of his family, and he transformed France into the superpower of its time. During Napoleon's coronation in 1804, Pope Pius VII handed Napoleon the crown, which Napoleon symbolically placed upon his own head. As he campaigned, conquering country after country, Napoleon gave crowns to his siblings, who ruled as monarchs within his empire: his older brother Joseph was crowned King of Naples and later King of Spain; his younger brother Louis was crowned King of Holland; his youngest brother Jérôme was crowned King of Westphalia; and his sisters Elisa, Pauline and Caroline each became an Imperial French Princess. His achievements for himself, his family and France were unprecedented.

Out of fear of God, the Vatican, or the Vatican's many powerful defenders, most people would usually do what the Pope said without question. Not only did Napoleon openly question – and publicly quarrel with – multiple popes, in 1809 he had Pope Pius VII (the same pope from his coronation) kidnapped and imprisoned over a disagreement.

The early years

Napoleon was born in Corsica, a Mediterranean island that belongs to France, just north of Italy's Sardinia. He was raised speaking an Italian dialect known as Corsican. During his later childhood, his family moved to mainland France where he became fluent in French. It is worth remembering that he was always considered to be an outsider to the French aristocracy as he never fully lost his Corsican accent. With an accent that was commonly ridiculed, he gave dramatic speeches and proclamations to native French soldiers and aristocracy alike.

Napoleon's formative years took place during a time of repeated political instability in France. With political instability comes power vacuums, which create the opportunity to amass authority. One of Napoleon's defining moments was the Battle of Toulon, where he dramatically recaptured the town from the British Empire, then the largest in the world.

Napoleon rose through the ranks of the French military and eventually began overthrowing and conquering kingdom after kingdom, obliterating ancient hierarchies and outdated power structures. Even as emperor, Napoleon actively took his place on the battlefield. Not only did he stand by his troops and make his presence known, he also gave speeches. He was one of the few people in history who fought with both sword and pen.

While Chinggis Khan's power was dependent on the support of his warlords, Napoleon's power hinged on the love and loyalty of his troops. Napoleon's unique position as emperor and general is reflected in his many direct orations and proclamations to his troops. In these messages, he would usually do one of three things:

1. Tell his soldiers how great they were (usually either before or after an important battle)
2. Tell his soldiers that they were a disgrace to France and should be ashamed of themselves (usually after they performed badly in a battle)
3. Tell his soldiers that they should worship him (consistent at all times)

Almost all of Napoleon's addresses are characterised by an overwhelming outpouring of emotions and an abundance of repetition for emphasis.

Napoleon's emotive repetition

Napoleon understood that the best way to motivate people was by stirring their emotions. In May 1796, Napoleon and his troops managed to capture the city of Milan from the Holy Roman Empire. For Napoleon, who was not yet given the title Emperor, this was another momentous occasion. He told his troops:

> **Soldiers:** You have rushed like a torrent from the top of the Apennines; you have overthrown and scattered all that opposed your march. [...] The army which so proudly threatened you can find no barrier to protect it against your courage; neither the Po,

> the Ticino, nor the Adda could stop you for a single day. These vaunted bulwarks of Italy opposed you in vain; you passed them as rapidly as the Apennines. These great successes have filled the heart of your country with joy.

Napoleon congratulated his soldiers with a simile comparing them to the mighty destructive forces of nature. Chinggis Khan used a very similar metaphor when he spoke of his men as his 'four dogs,' 'smashing the cliffs' and 'cutting the deep waters in two'. Both spoke to troops after battle, both used the forces of nature as a metaphor, and both used the metaphor to build support from their soldiers. However, as I mentioned earlier, the main difference is that Napoleon – serving in a perhaps more egalitarian society than Chinggis Khan – was addressing his troops, while Chinggis was addressing his chieftains. In saying these things, both generals use a very similar variant of *comprobatio* to elicit pride from their men.

Similarly to Attila the Hun's war speech against the Western Roman Empire and the Visigoths, Napoleon used *argumentum ad hominem* when he emphasised the enemy's pride. The first example of this is when he said they 'proudly threatened you', and the second was when he called them 'vaunted bulwarks' (meaning: overconfident defensive walls). This *argumentum ad hominem* would have likely been used to magnify the feeling of victory: it emphasised the *pathos*.

Towards the end of the extract, Napoleon personified the state of France with a heart filled with joy. This is another example of *pathos*. Any references to the 'heart' or to 'joy' are usually always intended to provoke an emotive response from the listener.

Later on in the speech (not included in the extract), to really hammer home the feeling of pride, Napoleon said that that pride would come from 'your fathers, your mothers, your wives, sisters, and mistresses'. By listing all of the family members with this use of *abundantia*, Napoleon emphasised that everyone would be proud of them. It is possible that he even did so with a cheeky use of humour when alluding to the possibility that his troops would have mistresses as well as wives. Through the use of *abundantia*, Napoleon used pride as a reward, which he is showering onto the soldiers.

It is interesting to note that, in the same speech, Napoleon used pride as a vice when he spoke of the enemy, but a virtue in the hearts of his own people.

Napoleon wanted his troops to feel pride so that he could motivate them to win more battles. Ultimately, this objective was to win the next battle, not just to celebrate the current. As with all tyrants, generosity usually has an end goal. That being the case, it makes sense that, after hyping their emotions with *pathos*, Napoleon spoke about the future: his ambitions and expectations:

> We have still forced marches to make, enemies to subdue, laurels to gather, injuries to revenge. Let those who have sharpened the daggers of civil war in France, who have basely murdered our ministers, and burnt our ships at Toulon, tremble!

Similarly to Goebbels and Mark Antony in the Introduction, Napoleon riled up his soldiers for battle, exciting them with the prospect of bloody revenge. By describing the enemy as 'those who have sharpened the daggers of civil war in France, who have basely murdered our ministers, and burnt our ships at Toulon,' Napoleon used a *tricolon of argumentum ad hominem*. By listing three villainous things the enemy had done immediately after inflating their egos with pride, Napoleon would have excited his troops with a desire for further military glory. You can almost picture the excitement of his soldiers – who believe themselves to be 'like a torrent from the top of the Apennines' – when their leader says they will make the enemies of their nation 'tremble'.

Already, from this short extract, we can see how the mighty Napoleon used rhetoric to elicit emotions from his army. But it wasn't all sunshine and roses with the emperor.

On occasion, Napoleon gave speeches to scold his troops. Later that year, at Mantua (another Italian town under the rule of The Holy Roman Empire), Napoleon's troops were forced to abandon their siege. For Napoleon, abandoning a siege would have been akin to failure. Napoleon lambasted his troops with the same fervent passion that he praised them. He said:

> Soldiers: I am not satisfied with you; you have shown neither bravery, discipline, nor perseverance; no position could rally you; you abandoned yourselves to a panic-terror; you suffered yourselves to be driven from situations where a handful of brave men might have stopped an army. Soldiers of the 39th and 85th, you are not French soldiers. Quartermaster-general, let it be inscribed on their colours, 'They no longer form part of the Army of Italy!'

One of the things to note in this speech is the extent to which Napoleon used repetition to emphasise his disapproval of the troops. By saying that they had shown 'neither bravery, discipline, nor perseverance', Napoleon used a *tricolon of abundantia*. The *anaphoric* repetition of 'you' further directed Napoleon's fury at the soldiers themselves. There was also a new form of repetition in this scolding which we haven't encountered yet: *anadiplosis*. *Anadiplosis* is when a word at the end of a sentence is repeated as the opening of the next sentence. Napoleon used this when he said, 'no position could rally you; you abandoned yourselves to a panic-terror'. *Anadiplosis* can be a very effective rhetorical repetition for either emphasising a point, or making logical links in an argument.

Napoleon then used another exciting rhetorical feature called *apostrophe*. *Apostrophe* is when a speaker changes the intended audience of their words mid-speech. In this extract, Napoleon stopped addressing his troops and began to address the quartermaster. *Apostrophe* is a very powerful rhetorical tool because it turns your audience into spectators. When a speaker changes who they are talking to, it tends to make their speeches sound more ceremonial and often reengages the audience. While Napoleon was giving the quartermaster a genuine order, he made a point of giving it publicly in front of the troops. This would have been done to emphasise their shame. Napoleon was technically speaking to the quartermaster, but it was the 39th and 85th who were the intended recipients of his words.

In his attempts to illicit shame, Napoleon was once more using *pathos*; but in a very different manner.

After this glitch at the Siege of Mantua, Napoleon returned and captured the city: he lost the battle but won the war.

Kairos and ethos

You can find many character similarities between rulers such as Napoleon, Julius Caesar, and Chinggis Khan: all three of these men managed to make themselves the most powerful man on earth; each had to consolidate his position of power; each had to establish his *ethos*; each attempted to do this through references to divinity.

Whilst Napoleon had a certain way he would speak to his troops about battles, he had another tone for when he was speaking about himself: an imperious one. This can be seen when he addressed his troops after the War of the Third Coalition in October 1805. Napoleon, now crowned Emperor, had just defeated an army of 100,000 men; 60,000 of them, including many enemy generals, were captured as prisoners. The Third Coalition, whom Napoleon had just defeated in battle, was made up of the collective empires of Britain, Austria, Russia, as well as the kingdoms of Naples and Sicily. This was the first major conflict of the Napoleonic Wars.

When speaking of the resounding victory, to bolster his own status and promote himself as an unprecedented strategist, Napoleon said:

> [...] I was enabled to secure the wished-for result without incurring any danger, and, what is unexampled in the history of nations, that result has been gained at the sacrifice of scarcely fifteen hundred men killed and wounded.

Why is Napoleon publicly praising himself in front of his troops? Because he wants them to believe that he is the best general in the world: that he is the man to lead them. He emphasised this through the use of *kairos*. By saying that what he had achieved was 'unexampled in the history of nations', Napoleon stated that he had achieved what no one throughout all of time has managed to achieve. In short: he was better than all of the rulers of history.

Immediately after saying this, to close this address, Napoleon said:

> Soldiers: this success is due to your unlimited confidence in your Emperor, to your patience in enduring fatigues and privations of every kind, and to your singular courage and intrepidity.

This might seem over the top and exaggerated, but in 1805, Napoleon's soldiers would have probably loved every word. His praise for the soldiers was further emphasised by a *tricolon of anaphora* at the final three clauses – all of which began with 'to'.

I briefly mentioned Napoleon's use of *kairos* in his military address in 1805. In 1808, when praising his troops before their battle in Spain, he again used this technique when he said:

> Soldiers: You have passed the renown of our modern armies, but you have not yet equalled the glories of those Romans, who, in one and the same campaign, were victorious upon the Rhine and the Euphrates, in Illyria and upon the Tagus. A long peace, a lasting prosperity, shall be the reward of your labours. But a real Frenchman ought not, could not, rest until the seas are open to all. Soldiers: All that you have done, all that you will do for the happiness of the French people, and for my glory, shall be eternal in my heart.

In true dictatorial style, Napoleon invoked the past glory of the Roman empire to motivate his troops to rouse them to fight even more. Without explicitly mentioning time, Napoleon used his place on the timeline of history to motivate his troops to compete with an ancient empire. Many dictators have invoked Roman imagery and language when establishing their own glorious *ethos*. Napoleon would often be portrayed in art with golden laurels – another homage to the emperors of Rome.

Napoleon's pride came before a fall. In 1806, he began a series of counter-productive economic sanctions against his nemesis: the British Empire. Napoleon ordered a full continental blockade. This meant that all kingdoms under Napoleon's rule were banned from trading with Britain. In Emperor Napoleon's own words: 'I will no longer tolerate a single English envoy in Europe; I will declare war on any power that has one.'

While this blockade did harm the British economy, it devastated the economies of the many kingdoms in Napoleon's empire. The blockade meant that they were starved of British goods such as sugar, coffee, cocoa, tobacco, and cotton textiles: all key trading commodities at the time. Many historians view this as the turning point in Emperor Napoleon's popularity and power.

After having to quash a revolt in Spain (1807-1814), Napoleon then mounted a catastrophic invasion of Russia (1812 – 1814). Despite having captured Moscow, Napoleon and his soldiers had to retreat from the ruthless winter, which inflicted mass desertion and death on the French forces.

The defeat robbed Napoleon of his strongest weapon: his popularity. Unlike the Tsars of Russia and the other Royal families of the Continent, in post-revolutionary France Napoleon relied on his reputation among ordinary people and especially his troops. He reputedly told an Austrian nobleman:

> Your sovereigns who were born to their thrones cannot comprehend the feelings that move me. To them it is nothing to return to their capitals defeated. But I am a soldier. I need honour and glory. I cannot reappear among my people devoid of prestige. I must remain great, admired, covered with glory.

When Napoleon returned from his failed Russian invasion devoid of prestige and glory, in 1814, he was forced to abdicate. He was exiled to the Mediterranean island of Elba, where he ruled as 'emperor' of its 12,000 inhabitants.

Less than a year later, however, in March 1815, Napoleon managed to escape Elba and return to France. As he was marching back to Paris, more and more soldiers joined him. One anecdote suggests that when Napoleon was confronted by troops tasked with stopping him, he opened his coat jacket and said to them: 'If any of you will shoot his Emperor, here I am'. Instead of shooting him, they joined his march on Paris. By the time he reached Paris, he had amassed a great army.

It was to this army, while marching to Paris, that he said the following:

> Soldiers: Come and range yourselves under the banners of your chief; his existence is only made up of yours; his rights are only those of the people and yours; his interest, his honour, his glory, are no other than your interest, your honour, and your glory. Victory shall march at a charging step; the eagle, with the national colours, shall fly from steeple to steeple, till it reaches the towers of Notre Dame. Then you will be able to show your scars with honour; then you will be able to boast of what you have done; you will be the liberators of the country! In your old age, surrounded and looked up to by your fellow citizens, they will listen to you with respect as you recount your high deeds, you will each of you be able to say with pride, 'And I also made part of that grand army which entered twice within the walls of Vienna, within those of Rome, of Berlin, of Madrid, of Moscow, and which delivered Paris from the stain which treason and the presence of the enemy had imprinted on it.' Honour to those brave soldiers, the glory of their country!

In this dramatic speech of a returning hero, you can see Napoleon using a host of rhetorical features to make his return as glorious as possible. Napoleon was once more praising his troops, and using an abundance of repetition. He emphasised that he owed everything to his troops when he repeated 'yours' at the end of his sentences. This form of repetition (at the end of sentences or clauses) is known as *epistrophe*. There is also a persuasive *tricolon* for emphasis in the anaphoric repetition of 'his interest, his honour, his glory' which was mirrored with 'your interest, your honour, and your glory'.

Napoleon then painted a picture of all the glory they would receive if they helped him successfully reclaim Paris. Like so many dictators, Napoleon was once more selling his followers a dream they could live for, fight for, and die for.

The End of Napoleon

After this dramatic speech, Napoleon successfully entered Paris, overpowered the political rebellion that banished him, and was reinstated as Emperor of France. With his return to power also came the return of the Napoleonic Wars. His enemies, in this instance made up mostly by Britain and Prussia, formed the Seventh Coalition and marched against the reinstated French Emperor.

Only three months after returning to power, Napoleon faced a momentous battle: the Battle of Waterloo on Sunday 18 June 1815. A series of misfortunes plagued Napoleon. So much rain fell that the ground was transformed into a thick layer of mud. This meant that Napoleon's cannons, on which his military strategy depended, became unmaneuverable. To add to this, Napoleon was suffering from poor health. Severe constipation meant that he couldn't ride his horse to see what was happening during the battle; he couldn't think clearly because of the pain, and he had to rely on the strategy of lesser men.

In defeat, Napoleon, the mighty emperor once famed in glorious victory, was shipped by the British to exile on St Helena, a small island under British control in the middle of the Atlantic Ocean with extreme heat in summer and dampness in winter. Six years into his banishment, at the age of 51, he died, reportedly from a stomach ulcer. In 1840, Napoleon's body was relocated from St Helena to Paris, where it currently lies in one of the grandest tombs in Europe.

During his energetic and bloody reign, religious freedoms flourished, a proper education system was established, and a fairer and more universal legal system was put in place throughout France and parts of Europe.

His success lay in his unceasing ambition and his military genius. Both were underpinned by his use of rhetoric: he was a master of public speaking. Whether it was telling his troops off as a young general or praising them as an emperor, Napoleon used an abundance of rhetorical features to persuade his soldiers to march for his personal glory and build him the greatest European empire the world had ever seen.

Ranavalona I (1778-1861).
Philippe-Auguste Ramanankirahina (1860-1915).
Photograph of the original work displayed at the Lapan'
Andafiavaratra (Antananarivo).

7.
RANAVALONA I

We are now moving forward in time from Napoleon but only by a few decades, and to a part of the world which is shrouded in mystery, steeped in tradition, and relatively unknown to the history books with which most of us are familiar: Madagascar, the fourth largest island on earth.

Situated off the coast of southeast Africa, Madagascar has a land mass greater than France, sandy beaches, exotic jungles, and a rich tribal history. In part due to its geographic isolation, it managed to remain free from European colonisation until the very end of the 19th century when it was finally taken over by France.

While a large part of Madagascar's pre-colonisation history is unknown, the little that we have is worth exploring.

Ranavalona I

Of particular interest is a 19th century Malagasy queen, Queen Ranavalona I, who, through various policies including ruthless judicial reforms, was responsible for killing 50 per cent of her own people. In the early years of her reign, she reduced the population of Madagascar from 5 million to 2.5 million. She became known as The Mad Queen of Madagascar.

Ranavalona I came to power in 1828 following the death of her husband, King Radama I. With some political foul play, she steamrolled over the dynastic procedure and asserted herself as absolute ruler. At the time, the royal tradition was, after ascending to the throne, the new sovereign hunted down and killed all political rivals. Ranavalona did a good job of this; among her first victims was her nephew, Rakotobe (the late king's eldest sisters' eldest son and the rightful heir according to the line of succession).

The Coronation Speech

As monarch, the first thing Ranavalona had to do was consolidate her *ethos*, justify her position in power, and reassure the people that their fears and concerns were meaningless. And what is the best way to do that? A speech, of course.

On 12 July 1828, Princess Ranavalona was made Queen in a grand coronation ceremony at which she addressed 60,000 people (including 8,000 soldiers).

We are lucky here that William Ellis, a Christian missionary, spent a good amount of time living in Madagascar and documented the procession, the flags of the idols on which the monarch had to pray, and the palanquin (a form of transport in which one person sits in a luxurious box which is carried by four or more men). Ranavalona's palanquin, which was ceremoniously paraded to the palace, was decorated with 'scarlet cloth richly adorned with gold lace', as was her throne. Armed soldiers paraded in huge numbers, military bands performed for the crowd, and cannons were fired in a resplendent display of grandeur.

His account offers the world a rare insight into a corner of history that would otherwise be completely unknown, partly because Ranavalona I killed most of the other Europeans who might have documented these sorts of occasions. This is what we have of her speech (with a few side notes from Ellis):

> 'Veloma Zanadralambo, veloma Zanakandriandroraka, veloma Zanakandriamasinavalona, (I salute you, different clans named)', and continued, 'If you have never known me before, it is I, Ranavalona, who now appear[s] before you.' The people shouted 'Hoo, hoo.' Then she said, 'God gave the kingdom to my ancestors, they transferred it Andriampoinimerina, and he again to Radama, on condition that I should be his successor. Is it not so, Ambaniandro?' – (my subjects). All replied, 'It is so.' Again she added, 'I will not change what Radama and my ancestors have done; but I will add to what they did. Do not think that because I am a woman, I cannot govern the kingdom: never say, she is a woman weak and ignorant, she is unable to rule over us. My greatest solicitude and study will always be to promote your welfare, and to make you happy. Do you hear that, Ambaniandro?' All replied, 'Yes.'

After this, her Prime Minister reportedly said a few words. This is all we have of Ranavalona's coronation speech.

The opening sentence in which she saluted the three tribes presents us with an *anaphoric tricolon of comprobatio* (compliments to the tribes). As a new ruler, she needed support; as we know, people are more likely to support you if you are nice to them. It is hard to avoid the similarities between this ceremonial speech and Chinggis Khan and Napoleon's flattery of their soldiers and generals.

The Mad Queen of Madagascar then immediately went on to present her *ethos* and justify her right to rule by claiming that the previous kings were her ancestors (technically, they weren't, because she married into the family).

One of the interesting features of this speech is the explicit audience engagement. There are instances where the audience chanted 'Hoo, hoo' to express their approval of her message, but there are also moments where she addressed the audience directly with a question, which they answered.

She asserted that she was the rightful successor – a claim that is generally thought to be untrue – and then said: 'Is it not so, my subjects?' One might argue that it takes a lot of bravery to make a statement like that and subsequently call your audience 'my subjects'. Whether it was out of bravery, arrogance, or a combination of the two, it worked. It is possible that the audience response was scripted: perhaps the audience was briefed before; or perhaps the wording of the speech was ceremonial and therefore known. It is also possible that it was a genuine response. Unlike more recent speeches which were broadcast or reported on in newspapers, her audience consisted solely of the people present. There was no mass media to report on the story to a secondary audience: no newspapers or cinema screenings.

It is important to distinguish Ranavalona's use of questions to the more traditional rhetorical questions. While rhetorical questions require no response from the audience, Ranavalona's questions require a very specific response from her audience. She asks two questions in her coronation speech: 'Is it not so, Ambaninandro?' and 'Do you hear that, Ambaniandro?' Ambaniandro is a collective noun which, in this example, referred to the audience. Both of her questions are to prompt her audience to agree with her and/or express their understanding.

After the theatrical call and response with the audience, Ranavalona directly addressed the elephant in the room: the fact that she was a woman. She didn't give a counter argument that she was able, or that women could govern just as well as men, she simply told (or possibly warned) her audience not to question her.

It is hard not to draw comparisons between this speech and Elizabeth I's address to her soldiers at the Tilbury where she said: 'I know I have the body of a weak, feeble woman; but I have the heart and stomach of a king, and of a king of England too'. Both queens asserted their *ethos* to their predominantly (presumably) male-dominated audiences with strong statements. While Ranavalona used imperative warnings, Elizabeth used a powerful *antithesis* (contrasting her weak body and her kingly heart and stomach). Both acknowledged their audiences' reservations about their genders and confronted them directly. It is fascinating to think that, despite being separated by continent, culture, religion, language, and centuries, both these queens had a united message, which was derived from their gender and their audience's prejudice.

Queen Ranavalona I then said: 'My greatest solicitude and study will always be to promote your welfare, and to make you happy'. As we have seen time and time again, tyrants tell their audiences what they want to hear. They present the *ethos* which will win the favour of the audience, irrespective of whether that *ethos* is in any way true to their character. Had the newly crowned Queen Ranavalona I stood up and said: 'I plan to kill half of you' we can assume her audience would have demurred.

Ranavalona managed to successfully assert her *ethos* as the new and undisputed monarch of Madagascar. She was free to wield her power and do as she wished, with little to no consequences. While we don't have many speeches, we do have some of her edicts, which Ellis documented in his publications.

The Anti-Christianity edict

As a Malagasy traditionalist, Queen Ranavalona I was not a fan of outside thinking. The biggest form of outside thinking that affected her kingdom was Christianity. The growth of Christianity was a threat to the Malagasy way of life that was so dear to her. The Malagasy people were banned from practising Christianity and, by the mid-1830s, most foreigners had left Madagascar. As part of her efforts to preserve the Malagasy customs, Ranavalona issued a powerful edict.

Not only was the rhetoric significant, but so too was the ceremony that preceded it. Ellis noted:

> The morning of the day on which the people were to assemble, was ushered in by the firing of cannon, for the purpose of exciting fear in the minds of the people, and impressing them with a sense of the importance attached by the government to the transactions of the day.
>
> When the people assembled, about 15,000 troops under arms were marched to the place, with a view of showing the ability and determination of the government to enforce its wishes. At the appointed time the chief military officers and the judges appeared, and delivered the queen's edict which was announced by the judges, and enforced by the military officers.

The edict opened:

> I announce to you, O ye Ambaniandro, I am not a sovereign that deceives, nor are the servants deceived. I, therefore, announce to you what I purpose to do, and how I shall govern you. Who then is that man, a servant too, that would change the customs of our ancestors, and the twelve sovereigns in this country? To whom has the kingdom been left by inheritance, by Impoinimerina and Radama, except to me? If then, any would change the customs of our ancestors, and of the twelve sovereigns, I abhor that, saith Rabodo-nandrian-impoinimerina.
>
> Now, on the subject of revelling the idols, treating the divination as a trifle, and throwing down the tombs of the Vazimba; I abhor that, saith Ranavalomanjaka. Do it not in my country. The idols (say you) are nothing. By them, it is that the twelve kings have been established; and now are they changed, to become 'nothing'? The divination also you treat in the same manner; and the tombs of the Vazimba, indeed, are their evidence. Even the sovereign counts them sacred; and are the people to esteem them as 'nothing'? This is my affair, saith Ranavalomanjaka, and I hold them guilty, whoever in my country destroys them, (the tombs).

In this edict, Ranavalona used a rhetorical technique called *elenchus*. *Elenchus* refers to when a speaker uses a series of rhetorical questions for the purpose of refuting an argument. The most famous use of elenchus in Western culture is the speech of Shylock in Shakespeare's *Merchant of Venice* which reads:

> Hath not a Jew eyes? Hath not a Jew hands, organs, dimensions, senses, affections, passions? Fed with the same food, hurt with the same weapons, subject to the same diseases, healed by the same means, warmed and cooled by the same winter and summer, as a Christian is? If you prick us, do we not bleed? If you tickle us, do we not laugh? If you poison us, do we not die? And if you wrong us, shall we not revenge?

While Queen Ranavalona I used *elenchus* in both paragraphs, in the first paragraph she used it to make a point about her character and right to rule (thus, a use of *ethos*), and, in the second paragraph, she used *elenchus* to argue against the move away from traditional Malagasy divination.

Some might interpret her use of rhetorical questions in this extract as *epiplexis* – when a speaker asks a series of rhetorical questions to berate, blame, or elicit an emotional response from an audience.

Ranavalona's argument against moving away from traditional practices was emphasised through her application of *epistrophe* when she repeated 'nothing' at the end of her rhetorical questions in the second paragraph. One can imagine the emphasis placed on the 'nothing' was designed to shock the audience at the sacrilegious nature of the affront to their customs. When a speaker invokes tradition and culture it triggers an emotional response in our identity. Even if the people hearing this edict had moved away from that ideology, they would have memories of it. By invoking those emotive parts of the audience's identity and then slamming them as 'nothing', Ranavalona would have stirred some patriotism, sadness, or perhaps even anger amongst her people.

Ranavalona's mighty use of *pathos* was introduced with a powerful *tricolon* where, likely with the intention of enraging her audience, she listed the sacrilegious acts and then stated her own opinion. This was when she said: 'Now, on the subject of revelling the idols, treating the divination as a trifle, and throwing down the tombs of the Vazimba; I abhor that'. The three points of sacrilege in this sentence would no doubt have been intended to outrage the traditionalists in her society. One can imagine that even those who may have been sympathetic to Christian thinking would have shuddered.

The rest of the edict specified that anyone who attended a missionary school, attended places of worship, or had any cultural influence from Christianity needed to 'confess'.

There was further use of *elenchus* in the edict, as it continued:

> As to baptism, societies, places of worship, distinct from schools, and the observances of the Sabbath, how many rulers are there in this land? Is it not I alone that rule? These things are not to be done, they are unlawful in my country, saith Ranavalomanjaka; for they are not the customs of our ancestors, and I do not change their customs, excepting as to things alone which improve my country.
>
> Now then, those who have observed baptism, entered into society, and formed separate houses for prayer (or worship,) I grant you one month, saith Ranavalomanjaka to confess, (to make self-accusation,) and if you come not within that period, but wait to be first found out, accused by others, I denounce death against such for I am not a sovereign that deceives, and servants are not to be deceived. Make then the time, it is one month from yonder sun of the Sabbath, that I gave you to confess, and this is the method you are to adopt: The scholars at Ambodinandohalo, and those at Ambatonakanga, and not those

only, for there are scholars in all these twelve principal towns, and the scholars alone have worshipped and learned, – these are not condemned, and those are not to confess; but those who have opened other houses – these are to accuse themselves.

Ranavalona's explicit threat to kill anyone who didn't confess was reinforced by her use of *ethos* which was made by repeating: 'I am not a sovereign that deceives, and servants are not to be deceived'.

Later on in the edict she repeated it a third time when she proclaimed:

I, the sovereign, do not deceive, but if any come first, and accuse you, I denounce death against you, and I do not deceive, saith Ranavalomanjaka.

This threat also invoked the power of *kairos* (time). For anyone who engaged in Christian practices, the time to confess was immediately, else they risked a painful and excruciating death.

This edict can be interpreted as her justification for her traditional policies. By twisting the audience's emotions with these rhetorical techniques, Ranavalona was justifying her position, her actions, and her tyranny. This is an edict of a dictator who would commit atrocities against her own people and then dress it up as love, kindness, and tradition. Ellis wrote that after the edict: 'The powers of darkness were permitted to triumph'.

Judicial Reforms

Once she became undisputed monarch, Ranavalona I decided that Madagascar needed to go back to its golden era before being influenced by the West. When she assumed power, Madagascar was using a modern Western judicial system where people gathered, examined evidence, and passed judgement. Unhappy with this departure from Malagasy tradition, Ranavalona I reintroduced a traditional form of justice known as trial by ordeal. In trial by ordeal, the accused is put through a highly traumatic experience to see what happens, with the verdict decided by the outcome.

The traditional Malagasy trial by ordeal involved a native Malagasy plant known as the tangena shrub which is native to some coastal regions in Africa. The tangena shrub produces a highly toxic nut. If someone was accused of a crime such as witchcraft or Christian practices, they would have to swallow three pieces of chicken skin and then some poison made from the tangena shrub. There were three usual outcomes:

1. The accused died – this meant they were guilty.
2. The accused survived the poison and regurgitated all three pieces of chicken – this meant they were innocent.
3. The accused survived the poison and regurgitated fewer than three pieces of chicken skin – this meant they were guilty and would be killed.

Many Malagasy people believed that this ritual was highly accurate. Records show us that people were often keen to eat the poison to prove their innocence, often volunteering themselves for the ritual.

Combining the deadly justice system with plague and unnecessary war, the population of Madagascar plummeted.

Tyrant, fanatic, dictator, whatever term you choose to call her, Ranavalona I left her devastating mark on her island nation.

The End of The Mad Queen of Madagascar

Being a tyrannical dictator often ends with a violent and gory death, or a pathetic lonely demise exiled in a meaningless hellhole. In the case of Queen Ranavalona I, she managed to escape any gruesome fate or untimely death. She ruled for 33 years. After the turbulence of her early years when many died or were killed, things calmed down. She died peacefully in her sleep on 16 August 1861 and was succeeded by her son. The lucky 50 per cent of the population who survived her reign mourned her for nine months, as was the custom.

From the way she gained power to the way she wielded it, Queen Ranavalona I brought immense suffering and misery to the Malagasy people. Even in Madagascar, with a queen who rejected European values and cultures, we can see the same speeches, given in the same way, and achieving similar effects to so many others throughout the history of the world. No community, no matter how isolated, will ever be safe from the tyranny and oppression of the malice of rhetoric.

Benito Mussolini (1883-1945).
Portrait printed in the Italian magazine Tempoin 1939.

8.
MUSSOLINI

As we enter the 20th century, the construction and execution of the speeches remains mostly the same, but the scale of the audience rockets. With higher literacy levels, more people could read speeches in newspapers. With technological advances, more people could listen to speeches on the radio or watch them in their local cinema. The speeches were, essentially, the same, but the scale of their power was magnified to new heights the likes of which the world had never seen before.

When it came to political indoctrination, people were being manipulated faster and on a larger scale. Thanks to the well-documented nature or the time, we have a lot more content to discuss and fewer problems with source integrity.

After World War One, Italy was dejected. Many Italians died, and despite the vast quantities of Italian blood spilt, the post-war treaties denied Italy a lot of what she was promised. The economy was in ruins, and people felt that the political leadership was corrupt and weak. This led to depression, disgruntlement, and a desire for change.

In other words, it led to the perfect breeding ground for extremist ideologies and potential dictatorships. Enter Benito Mussolini.

Violent Little Benito's Rise to Power

There are many similarities between schoolteachers and dictators: a desire for ultimate control; a belief that they are the smartest person in the room; the knowledge that they can ruin people's lives with little to no consequence by making up and changing rules with little to no consistency.

Given the evident similarities, it may come as little surprise to learn that, before becoming the first fascist dictator of Europe, Benito Mussolini worked as a primary school teacher. Surprisingly, he was allowed to become a primary school teacher despite having twice stabbed fellow school pupils, once when he was 10 and a second time when he was 14.

So how did violent little Benito go on to become murderous Mussolini? His first step was to find people who supported his radical fascist political ideology. Once he found his people, he riled them up with speeches until they took up arms. Known as Blackshirts due to the colour of their uniform, they formed squads who, led by Mussolini, went around Italian cities terrorising anyone who disagreed with their political beliefs.

Fascist is often thrown around as a derogatory term, often on social media by people who don't know its precise definition. Derived from the Latin word 'fasces' which referred to a bundle of sticks tied together (sometimes with an axe), fascism is an ultra-national authoritarian political movement. Under fascist thinking, the government must have full control. And the role of the people is to enthusiastically do everything they are told; or, at the very minimum, never to step out of line. That line is drawn by an iron-fisted dictator with a powerful cult following. True dictatorships don't form overnight.

In 1921, Mussolini was elected to the Italian parliament as the head of his newly-founded National Fascist Party. Now with a political foothold in parliament, and a social foothold through his Blackshirt militia, Mussolini was beginning to wield his power against the communists in Italy by physically attacking their offices and representatives.

By this stage, Mussolini himself was wielding much of his power through the force of his unrelenting personality and square-jawed, bull-necked physicality. *The Observer*'s unnamed correspondent noted on 1 October 1922 Mussolini's raw power in a speech in Florence: 'His powerful head was thrown back, his stern eye fixed them all as one person'. The journalist wrote of Mussolini:

> He is a great speaker, not an orator. He dominates his audience more by sheer force of his volcanic personality, which is well under control, than by the force of his words. The young men in Italy, full of intense zest for life, and of truculent patriotism, would follow him anywhere at the lift of a finger.

The Italian Government at the time, perhaps afraid of a communist revolution, turned a blind eye to Mussolini's growing fascist threat, thinking that it was, for the time being, working in their favour. Until it wasn't. Mussolini and his Blackshirts became so powerful that even the relatively democratic government of Italy was powerless to stop them. Through violence and intimidation, the Blackshirts began degrading democratic institutions. Then, on 28 October 1922, they marched on Rome.

Luigi Facta, the extravagantly-mustachioed Prime Minister of Italy, wanted to declare a state of emergency to stop the siege of Rome. The declaration would have enacted martial law, thus allowing him to deploy the Italian army to stop Mussolini and his brutal militia. In order for Facta to do this, he required the signature of the Italian monarch, King Victor Emmanuel III. Victor Emmanuel III, supposedly fearing civil war and bloodshed, refused to sign the declaration of emergency. In a flustered state of protest, on 29 October, Facta resigned. The following day, 30 October, Mussolini was invited by Victor Emmanuel III to form a coalition government. Thus Mussolini became Prime Minister of Italy and also Interior Minister, giving him control of the police.

As Prime Minister and Interior Minister, Mussolini merged his Blackshirt paramilitary forces with the official Italian army, while simultaneously dismantling democratic structures. This meant that positions of power were given to those most faithful to him. Anyone problematic was swiftly removed.

For the first few years, Mussolini made efforts to appear as if he were operating a normal Italian government. Then, in 1925, he tore down the existing power structures of the Italian political system and replaced them with his own. The turning point was the silencing of a prominent socialist leader called Giacomo Matteotti in 1924. In a speech, Matteotti openly accused the fascist government of electoral fraud. Eleven days later he was murdered.

Matteotti's murder triggered a wave of anti-fascist sentiment, with parliamentary legislators seeming to take stances which suggested they would vote against some of Mussolini's fascist reform legislation.

The 'I'm in Charge' Speech

On 3 January 1925, Mussolini gave a speech to parliament where he essentially warned Italy that he was in charge and no one could stand in his way. The Italian Statute had an article (Article 47), which allowed any member of the parliament to call the Prime Minister before the High Court of Justice. Directly referring to this, Mussolini dared people to challenge him. He opened this historic speech by saying:

> Gentlemen!
>
> The speech I am going to make before you might not be classed as a parliamentary speech. It may be possible that, at the end, some of you will find that this speech is tied, even though a space of time has elapsed, to the one I pronounced in this same hall on November 16th. Such a speech can lead somewhere, but it cannot lead to a political vote. In any case let it be known that I am not looking for this vote. I do not want it; I have had plenty. Article 47 of the Statute says: 'The Chamber of the Deputies has the right to accuse the Ministers of the King and to bring them to face the High Court of Justice.' I formally ask if in this Chamber, or outside it, there is any one who wants to make use of Article 47?

Naturally, everyone, including King Victor Emmanuel III, remained silent. Either through fear, intimidation, or by some other means, no one dared make use of Article 47, no one dared to speak out against Mussolini.

After this, Mussolini went on to address the violence of the Fascists, which he described as being 'surgical, intelligent and chivalrous'. This *tricolon* of adjectives to describe violence was then contrasted to the violence of his enemies which he described as being 'unintelligent, passionate and stupid'. By categorising different forms of violence, he justified the violence of his Blackshirts.

Then, in what is considered to be the most significant part of this historic speech, Mussolini took all moral responsibility for everything that was done by the Fascists (which, we can assume includes the violence and the assassinations). In doing so, he essentially told all of Italy, and the world, that he was in charge. His exact words were:

> I declare here before this assembly, before all the Italian people, that I assume, I alone, the political, moral, historical responsibility for everything that has happened. If sentences, more or less maimed, are enough to hang a man, out with the noose! If Fascism has only been castor oil or a club, and not a proud passion of the best Italian youth, the blame is on me! If Fascism has been a criminal association, if all the violence has been the result of a determined historical, political, moral delinquency, the responsibility for this is on me, because I have created it with my propaganda from the time of our intervention in the War up to this moment.

People tend to interpret this part of the speech as Mussolini claiming responsibility for the assassination of Giacomo Matteotti. In many ways, not only was he accepting responsibility, but he was also asking: *so what?*

Following this provocative claim of responsibility, Mussolini claimed the Fascists were the victims of violence and disorder which was imposed by other political factions. Mussolini made a point of heavily emphasising the suffering of the Fascist supporters:

he spoke of how fascist supporters had been killed, sharing some gruesome details. In one anecdote, he heightened his use of *pathos* by mentioning how a 73-year-old Fascist supporter was killed by being thrown off a high wall. No doubt Mussolini intended to erase other people's outrage by expressing his own outrage.

This bombastic speech was closed with a threatening promise to bring Italy peace through violence. He said:

> When two elements are struggling, the solution is force. There never was any other solution in history, and never will be.
>
> Now I dare to say that the problem will be solved. Fascism, the Government and the Party, is at its highest efficiency. Gentlemen, you have deceived yourselves! You thought that Fascism was over because I was restraining it, that the Party was dead because I was holding it back. If I would use one one-hundredth part of the energy that I used to contain the Fascists, to unleash them…. Oh! You would see, you would see then…
>
> But there will be no need for that, because the Government is strong enough to completely and definitively suppress this Aventine sedition.
>
> Italy, Gentlemen, wants peace, wants tranquillity, wants work, wants calm; we will give it with love, if possible, or with force, if necessary. You can be sure that in the 48 hours following this speech the situation will be clarified in every corner. We all know that this is not a personal fancy, not lust for government, not base passion, but only infinite and powerful love for the Fatherland.

Historians tend to agree that this speech was the moment Mussolini came out of the dictatorial closet. In these words, Mussolini expressed his intentions to use violence to eliminate his enemies and grant Italy what he said was 'peace' and 'tranquillity'.

Laws were introduced that allowed for socialists to be imprisoned without trial, the death penalty was reinstated, and all cinemas were forced to play government propaganda films before screenings. Italy was now under his complete control, and no one, not even the King of Italy, could stand in his way.

Over the next two decades, Mussolini would wreck Italy.

The 'Let's Go To War' Speech

In October 1935, Mussolini sought to convince the people of Italy that, despite the international problems that it would cause, they should support an invasion of Abyssinia, in modern day Ethiopia.

In the fashion of a truly populist speech, Mussolini addressed his audience in a mighty manner. He opened with:

> Blackshirts of revolution, men and women of all Italy, Italians all over the world, beyond the mountains, beyond the seas, listen.

Such an opening is not used by someone who is going to announce a limp economic policy which has little relevance to the people. This is the opening of a grand speech to which everyone must listen. The address opened with an ascending *tricolon*, which begins with the smallest group, the Blackshirts, then escalates to Italians in Italy, and then finally to Italians all over the globe. The global relevance of his words was emphasised by the geographic *antithesis* of 'mountains' and 'seas'. By addressing them like this, Mussolini collectively called on their Italian identities. National identity is often used for its emotive unifying capacity during times of struggle – its ability to invoke *pathos*.

The final word of this opening sentence was the imperative command 'listen'. Dictators give orders.

Generally speaking, when telling your people to make great sacrifices – potentially including mass death within the population – you start evoking 'the hour', and how important 'the hour' is. Mussolini, no stranger to the rhetoric of populism and clearly aware of the power of *kairos*, did just that:

> A solemn hour is about to strike in the history of the country. Twenty million Italians are at this moment gathered in the squares of all Italy. It is the greatest demonstration that human history records. Twenty million, one heart alone, one will alone, one decision.

Not only did Mussolini call the hour 'solemn', but he also emphasised the importance of time by invoking the records of human history to highlight the greatness of what was happening.

The objective of the *kairos* here was to help him further embolden the *ethos* of the people. In that time of desperation, his survival depended on all Italians uniting, and a good way of achieving such a feat was through the metaphors that they were 'one'. The notion of a people being 'one' is common throughout many nations. Indeed, the motto for the United States of America – a motto found on many symbols of US national identity – is a good example. The Latin motto 'e pluribus unum' roughly translates to 'from the many one'. The act of emboldening or re-forging a national *ethos* is a powerful tool for any tyrant. It is for exactly that reason that Mussolini used a unified national identity as a rallying cry.

Mussolini emphasised that unified national identity with his *tricolon of anaphora*. He did this when he said: 'Twenty million, one heart alone, one will alone, one decision.' If you break this down to what Mussolini was really saying, you might conclude that it was: *if you do not support this decision, you are not Italian*. If you choose to interpret this as a use of implied *logos*, it would be classified as a hypothetical logical syllogism: a syllogism where the outcome is dependent on an 'if' factor.

What was the decision that all Italians were supposedly unified in supporting? He hadn't actually announced that just yet. After all, this was just the beginning of the speech. Before sharing a violent call to action, the rhetorical guidebook for dictators decrees that one must use *pathos*. Naturally, that is what Mussolini did:

> For many months the wheel of destiny and of the impulse of our calm determination moves toward the goal. In these last hours the rhythm has increased and nothing can stop it now.
>
> It is not only an army marching towards its goal, but it is 44 million Italians marching in unity behind this army. Because the blackest of injustices is being attempted against them, that of taking from them their place in the sun. When in 1915 Italy threw in her fate with that of the Allies, how many cries of admiration, how many promises were heard? But after the common victory, which cost Italy 600,000 dead, 400,000 lost, one million wounded, when peace was being discussed around the table only the crumbs of a rich colonial booty were left for us to pick up. For 13 years we have been patient while the circle tightened around us at the hands of those who wish to suffocate us.

Mussolini told his audience that they had suffered, he explicitly identified that suffering, and then spoke of the injustices that were attempted against them: namely, that they were prevented from exploiting colonisation.

Mussolini used the classic *antithesis* of light and dark when he spoke of the 'blackest of injustices' and the audience's 'place in the sun'. These types of binary tropes – the ones which are usually framed as *antithesis* – send clear messages to the audience. Universally, any person, no matter which part of the world they are from, will choose light over darkness. This is something which is programmed into our basic biological instinct to survive. Even in his speech justifying a completely unjust and unnecessary invasion of a foreign empire, Mussolini used that biological programming to manipulate his audience to win their support. Logically speaking, this form of false binary is known as a *false dichotomy*. A *false dichotomy* is when only two options are presented with no acknowledgement there is a middle ground.

Criticising the Allies from World War One, Mussolini used *argumentum ad hominem* with *erotema* when he said: 'When in 1915 Italy threw in her fate with that of the Allies, how many cries of admiration, how many promises were heard?' This rhetorical question acted to hype up the audience's sense of injustice which was then emphasised with the powerful *tricolon* of numbers that followed, '600,000 dead, 400,000 lost, one million wounded'. Invoking the dead will always stir emotions. This is especially true when members of the audience know of someone who had died and, with numbers this high, that would have likely included most people. Mussolini invoked suffering in a way which implied that their loss would have been for nothing, should Italy not get to exploit 'colonial booty'.

This is the point of the speech where Mussolini began to talk of the 'decision' which he mentioned at the opening of the speech. The decision to invade Abyssinia despite international calls for sanctions against Italy if it did so. Mussolini said:

> We have been patient with Ethiopia for 40 years. It is enough now.
>
> The League of Nations, instead of recognizing the rights of Italy, dares talk of sanctions, but until there is proof of the contrary, I refuse to believe that the authentic people of France will join in supporting sanctions against Italy. Six hundred thousand dead whose devotion was so heroic that the enemy commander justly admired them—those fallen would now turn in their graves.
>
> And until there is proof to the contrary, I refuse to believe that the authentic people of Britain will want to spill blood and send Europe into a catastrophe for the sake of a barbarian country, unworthy of ranking among civilised nations. Nevertheless, we cannot afford to overlook the possible developments of tomorrow.

Mussolini spoke of the 'authentic people' of Britain and France, perhaps, in an attempt to suggest that Italy had popular support, despite almost unanimous condemnation from international political leaders. The implication of a split between the authentic people and political leadership has been a common trope trotted out by populist speakers. Highlighting the divide between the traditional political structures and the authentic people is often used by alternative politicians stoking the fires of extremism, making it a textbook favourite of dictators.

Harking back to the will of the authentic people can be interpreted as a use of *argumentum ad populum*. *Argumentum ad populum* is when a speaker argues that something is true based on who agrees with it (or how many people agree with it). The *argumentum ad populum* used here granted Mussolini's argument validity, thus negating opposition from political leaders and the League of Nations.

The vilification of Abyssinia can be seen as a further justification of the invasion through *argumentum ad hominem*: by calling Abyssinia a 'barbarian country, unworthy of ranking among civilised nations'. Mussolini and his regime placed great emphasis on vilifying Abyssinia because if you hurt bad people, the world doesn't judge you as harshly. The worse he made the Abyssinian empire look, the less people would object to his planned invasion.

The speech then reached a climax when Mussolini, in one sentence, threw out two *tricolons*, *anaphora*, and also *isocolon*:

> To economic sanctions, we shall answer with our discipline, our spirit of sacrifice, our obedience. To military sanctions, we shall answer with military measures. To acts of war, we shall answer with acts of war.

A country threatened by larger global powers is comforted by having a strong leader who demonstrates and promises strength. By casting an *ethos* of resolute conviction and authority, Mussolini would have inspired the same conviction in his audience. In the eyes of many Italians the message was clear: he would bring justice and glory to Italy, no matter the cost.

Later, towards the closing of the speech, Mussolini once more invoked *kairos* (again emphasising the strength of the Italian *ethos*):

> Never, as at this historical hour, have the people of Italy revealed such force of character, and it is against this people to which mankind owes its greatest conquest, this people of heroes, of poets and saints, of navigators, of colonisers, that the world dares threaten sanctions.

The implication behind this is that the world owes Italy the spoils of empire and that Italy deserves the spoils of empire. The *abundantia* which harks back to the great cultural contributions that Italy had made throughout history was a form of *ethos* which reinforced Mussolini's argument of entitlement; thus, reinforcing his *logos* – the argument that Italy is entitled and justified to exploit Abyssinia.

Immediately after this, to close his speech, Mussolini threw at his audience the rallying cry, the call to action, the order to embrace war:

> Italy! Italy! Entirely and universally Fascist! The Italy of the Blackshirt Fascist revolution, rise to your feet; let the cry of your determination rise to the skies and reach our soldiers in East Africa. Let it be a comfort to those who are about to fight. Let it be an encouragement to our friends and a warning to our enemies. It is the cry of Italy which goes beyond the mountains and the seas out into the great world. It is the cry of justice and of victory.

In the climactic conclusion of the speech, Mussolini began using short sentences to create tension and rhythm. Short sentences can give the impression of urgency and spontaneity: things that Mussolini would have wanted in that moment. When a speaker uses *kairos*, the sentences tend to get shorter.

The immediate repetition of 'Italy! Italy!' is a common rhetorical feature called *epizeuxis*: the immediate repetition of a word or phrase for emphasis and perhaps also the perception of authenticity.

Structurally, the speech followed a cyclical pattern. This means that the end of the speech replicated a theme or motif from the beginning. In Mussolini's case, it was the natural imagery of 'the mountains and the seas'.

The End of Mussolini

Mussolini gave many thundering speeches which shook the mountains and the seas. He brought tyranny and violence onto the people of Italy and involved them in wars they were doomed to lose.

During World War Two, the Italian economy ground to a halt. Factories halted production due to shortages of raw materials and people began to starve. As well as this, there was an increased German presence in Italy, which many Italians resented.

Mussolini ruled in Italy until 1943 when he was voted out by the Grand Council – his own creation – and was placed under arrest by the orders of King Victor Emmanuel III. Two months into his arrest, Nazi forces, now at war with Italy, freed him, and installed him at the head of a puppet government in northern Italy. At this point, Italy was in a state of civil war. In the North, supported by the Nazis, Mussolini ruled the 'Italian Social Republic'. In the South, the Kingdom of Italy was still loyal to King Victor Emmanuel III and his new Prime Minister.

As the Nazis began losing the war on both the Eastern and Western fronts, support for the Italian Social Republic waned. This, in turn, led to the weakening of Mussolini's newfound nation. In April 1945,

Mussolini attempted to flee Italy. He was captured before he managed to leave the country and swiftly executed.

When a fallen dictator is executed by their own people, the results are often gruesome. Mussolini's corpse was beaten, mutilated, and desecrated by an angry mob. After being beaten beyond recognition, his body was hung upside down in Milan alongside the corpse of his mistress and some of his associates for all of Italy to see. The victims of dictators want to undo their image, and to desecrate an image requires more than just a simple death.

Mussolini is a good introduction to the tyrants and dictators of World War Two and beyond. Not only was he the first fascist dictator of Europe, he was also the first to truly harness populist rhetoric in the age of mass media. He set the standard for the language of evil – a standard used by many tyrants who followed. He may not have been a 'great orator,' but he knew well how to use the techniques of rhetoric – and he had the sheer force of personality to hammer home his message.

*Paul Joseph Goebbels (1897-1945).
Portrait taken in 1933 by photographer Heinrich Hoffmann.*

9.
JOSEPH GOEBBELS

What better case study into the rhetoric of evil and the speeches of tyranny than the Nazis?

When we discuss the rhetorical methods used by the Nazis, it is important to emphasise that they should serve a stark reminder of how people can twist the beauty of the spoken word for malicious ends. We shouldn't be impressed by the way Nazis used the spoken word to indoctrinate the people of Germany any more than we should be impressed by a school shooter with a good aim. To borrow the words of Dennis Globe from his book *The Art of Great Speeches*: 'A wall that stands up is a good wall, but if it surrounds a concentration camp it is an abomination. No speechwriter should ever use words to build up such a wall'.

The Nazi regime became the most rhetorically prolific movement of its age because its leaders saw the value and power of the spoken word. Because they saw the worth of rhetoric, they systematically applied it across their speeches and communication strategies.

In his book *Mein Kampf*, published in 1925, Adolf Hitler, leader of the Nazi party, claimed that writing would never be as powerful as the spoken word. He wrote:

> The knights of the pen and the literary snobs of today should be made to realize that the great transformations which have taken place in this world were never conducted by a goose quill. No. The task of the pen must always be that of presenting the theoretical concepts which motivate such changes. The force which has ever and always set in motion great historical avalanches of religious and political movements is the magic power of the spoken word. The broad masses of a population are more amenable to the appeal of rhetoric than to any other force.

Given Hitler's staunch belief in the power of the spoken word, it comes as little surprise that he and his cronies weaponised rhetoric on every platform that they could. They did so to the point where their propaganda speeches became unavoidable to any person in Germany with a working ear. At its peak, the Nazi party had over 20,000 local branches which would hold public meetings on special occasions. Even today, listening to local party leaders stumble and mutter their way through a poorly written speech is boring. Hitler and Goebbels knew that they couldn't trust these local leaders – potentially with the eloquence of buffoons – to deliver powerful speeches that said everything they wanted them to say. To circumvent this, the central Nazi party distributed scripts of speeches for local leaders to deliver. This way everyone heard variations of the same carefully crafted messages: messages that were designed to distort logic, sow the seeds of hate, and indoctrinate the German public.

The key behind the success of the rhetoric of the Third Reich can be summarised as:

- The ability to understand the audience and thus harness the emotions in the room
- The emphasis placed on time
- The simplicity of the messages and the one common enemy

The crux of Nazi rhetoric was the vilification of the Jewish people. This can be seen as a form of mass *argumentum ad hominem*. But even in this, Hitler believed in communicating this message in the simplest manner possible, so that there could be no hesitation or doubt. Aware of the power of a scapegoat, onto which all blame could be laid, Hitler said:

> Make even adversaries far removed from one another seem to belong to a single category. A speaker who attempts to persuade an audience by a complicated, developed argument, or by attacking multiple enemies, is doomed to fail.

Hitler and his regime did everything they could to heap maximum blame on the entirely innocent Jewish people of the world.

Who Was Joseph Goebbels?

People often think of Joseph Goebbels as the finger-wagging politician and don't know much of his surprising origins and personal life.

Goebbels was born on 29 October 1897 to an ordinary family: they were not rich, they were not upper class, and they were very Catholic. Goebbels was born with several disabilities including a club foot and lung problems. This meant that, when Germany was involved in the First World War and men of his age were given the honour of serving their country, Goebbels was deemed unsuitable to serve in the army and his services were rejected.

Goebbels studied at multiple universities and eventually, in 1921, got a PhD in literature from the University of Heidelberg. His PhD supervisors, and a number of his teachers to whom it is documented that he was friendly and grateful, were Jewish. After university, he attempted to write plays and novels. He was unsuccessful and was forced to take a soulless job as a bank clerk. Devastated at his failure, he quit his job and moved back in with his parents.

He began writing diaries at the age of 26, while unemployed and living at his parents' house. He noted that, when he was 13, he met his friend's stepmother and 'Eros awoke'. He documented, in detail, his sexual fantasies and conquests – his diaries included a system for documenting the number of times he had sex with a particular woman by adding a number next to her name increasing each time they had slept together.

His first diary, in which he began his writing career, came from one of his lovers, a lady called Else Janke. Their relationship was a turbulent one, and ultimately ended when Goebbels found out that her mother was Jewish – in his own words (from his diary): 'She told me her roots. Since then her charms were destroyed for me'. Despite writing this, he carried on seeing her intermittently for a number of years between and alongside his other affairs.

Another dramatic lover of his was with a higher-class German woman named Anka Stalherm whose parents very much objected to her relationship with Goebbels, a failed writer, whom they saw as a penniless nobody. When he was eventually rejected by her, he documented, in detail, his plans for suicide. His father, having learnt about his woes, gave him money to finish his university studies instead.

Records suggest that it was in 1924 that Goebbels became interested in the Nazi party and befriended Adolf Hitler. As time went on, his writings become more passionately antisemitic.

He and Hitler managed to take over Germany in 1933. Hitler was the Chancellor and Goebbels became the Minister of Public Enlightenment and Propaganda. Goebbels oversaw all cultural matters in Nazi Germany and his main job was to brainwash the people. He did just that. He masterfully gave some of the most dramatic speeches of his time. He would practise his enunciation and gestures before delivering them, and he would always calculate what his audience was thinking and how he could manipulate them into complete and utter intellectual submission.

It is perhaps worth noting that as Minister for Propaganda, Goebbels filmed lots of videos and movies which involved working with famous and beautiful actresses. Despite having married Magda Goebbels in 1931 and having become a father, Goebbels was known to make sexual advances to many of these women and, as the powerful figure that he now was, many of them were too scared to reject him.

The Total War Speech

To meaningfully understand why and how the rhetoric behind a speech is effective, it's crucial to understand the context, such as the audience, the time, the location, the speaker, and the preceding political events. Goebbels delivered his infamous *Total War* speech – the defining moment of his career – 18 days after the Nazis completely, unquestionably, and humiliatingly lost the Battle of Stalingrad to the Soviet Red Army.

Stalingrad was a vital city for both Nazi Germany and the Soviet Union. As well as being a major industrial transport hub on the Volga River, Stalingrad was named after the leader of the Soviet Union, Joseph Stalin. Not only was the name of the city symbolic, but so too was the status of the soldiers doing the fighting: the German 6th Army, the most decorated German army unit.

The Battle of Stalingrad began on 23 August 1942, and lasted, officially, until 2 February 1943. The battle involved five months of intense fighting with major losses on both sides. Collectively, an estimated 1.9 million troops died fighting for Stalingrad. The surviving German troops – an estimated 91,000 – surrendered to the Soviet Red Army. This was the destruction and death of the 6th Army: the pride of Germany's military was gone. The loss at Stalingrad was a major blow to the morale of the German people: a people who had never tasted defeat on this scale.

On 31 January, German radio announced the defeat at Stalingrad. Significantly, this was the first time that Hitler and his regime accepted that they had lost something and was the first sign that Germany faced serious threats. Eighteen days after this radio announcement, on 18 February 1943, Goebbels staged what was, by all accounts, his finest speech. During times of war, lives are lost, economies are weak, and all the positive aspects of life seem to fade. Goebbels stood before a Germany that was defeated, humiliated, and depressed. In a polished rhetorical stroke, he managed to turn spirits from dejection to determination.

Goebbels delivered his thundering Total War speech at the Sportpalast, the biggest meeting hall in Berlin, on 18 February 1943. The Sportpalast was commonly used for Nazi rallies and major gatherings:

Hitler is known to have delivered some of his key speeches there. The vast building could accommodate 14,000 people.

Perhaps the best example of the Nazis capitalising on the power of spoken rhetoric, Goebbels' one-hour-and-forty-nine-minute-long speech was broadcast in its entirety twice on German national radio and an adapted version was printed in major newspapers. Excerpts of the speech were played in movie theatres across Germany.

Despite having only been delivered once, there are several versions of this speech in circulation. This is because there is the speech Goebbels gave, and the speech that Goebbels had printed in the newspapers. While they are almost entirely identical, there are some small but historically significant differences which were made to the published transcript. The most important difference was a mild slip up in which Goebbels began saying the wrong word, and then corrected himself.

When speaking about Germany's response to the Jewish 'threat', Goebbels said that Germany would respond with *'radikalster Ausr...-schaltung'*. The reason this is significant is because Goebbels begins saying one word, hesitates for a fraction of a second and then says a different word. The word he began saying was *Ausrottung* – the German word for 'extermination'; the word he then said was *Ausschaltung* – the German word for 'exclusion'. At that moment, the senior Nazi official almost publicly confessed to the atrocities being committed by him and his regime.

Short Simple Sentences and the Power of Time

The *Total War* speech was very passionate and whipped the audience into a bloodthirsty frenzy. Whenever his speech reached an emotional climax, Goebbels used short sentences to deepen the emotional effect.

The first advantage to short simple sentences is that it makes a message clearer and therefore easier for people in the audience to understand. Speechwriters often say that a good speaker is a master of simplification and an enemy of simplicity.

The second, more significant advantage is that short simple sentences can create a sense of passionate authenticity. Short sentences are more likely to sound spontaneous whereas long sentences are more likely to sound scripted. Another advantage to short snappy sentences is that they give the speaker more opportunities to take breaths. Audiences, for one reason or another, are generally more likely to connect with a speaker if they can see them breathing normally. We are, after all, primal creatures, and breathing is the most basic human function that we all share. From the way a speaker flares their nostrils to the stare they give their audience, every inhale in a speech can be an opportunity for them to demonstrate their feelings and emotions. And feelings and emotions are contagious.

Here is an example of one of the emotional peaks from the *Total War* speech in which Goebbels used short sentences to hype his audience into a frenzy:

> The future of Europe hangs on our success in the East. We are ready to defend it. The German people are shedding their most valuable national blood in this battle. The rest of Europe should at least work to support us. There are many serious voices in Europe that have already realized this. Others still resist. That cannot influence us. If danger faced them alone, we could view their reluctance as literary nonsense of no significance. But the danger faces us all, and we must all do our share. Those who today do not understand that will thank us tomorrow on bended knees that we courageously and firmly took on the task.

The use of short sentences in this extract creates a rhythm and subsequent tension: they stir emotion. This use of *pathos* works because a short beating rhythm (in any language) echoes some very core human nature – for example, a heartbeat – usually causing audiences to respond in more emotional ways.

The *pathos* created by the rhythm is then emphasised with the choices of words and ideas. For example, 'blood' is always a powerful metaphor when speakers are using pathos. In this extract, Goebbels, while speaking about defending the successes in the East, said: 'The German people are shedding their most valuable national blood in this battle'. This is the sort of language which causes an audience to form a collective identity; in this case, the audience was part of the personified 'German people' that was losing its blood – an impassioned declaration which was heightened by the adjective 'valuable'.

As the audience started to think about the blood that had been lost – their families and friends who had fallen – they began to clap, to cheer, and to scream in approval. If you have never experienced it, it is hard to explain the energy of being in a crowd with a hyper audience when raw emotions reverberate and ricochet across the room, indoctrinating the minds of the people who are part of the hypnotic sensation. It is when an audience is like this, energised and emotional, that a speaker can get them to do anything. This is why Goebbels hyped his audience, this is why he chose to give such an emotional speech, and this is why his next move was to present them with a passionate call to action. However, he was not speaking to soldiers, he was speaking to the doctors, to the teachers, to the shop owners, to the retired: he was speaking to everyone at home.

He went on and said:

> We pay no heed to class or standing. Rich and poor, high and low must share the burdens equally. Everyone must do his duty in this grave hour, whether by choice or otherwise. We know this has the full support of the people. We would rather do too much rather than too little to achieve victory. No war in history has ever been lost because of too many soldiers or weapons. Many, however, have been lost because the opposite was true.

Here, Goebbels told his audience that no one was exempt from the war effort and total war meant that everyone was involved; everyone made sacrifices, and everyone suffered for the greater victory. This message was emphasised through Goebbels' use of *antithesis* with 'rich and poor, high and low'. Technically, 'rich and poor, high and low' is a couplet of antithesis and, as the two clauses are of a similar length, it is also a use of *isocolon* (when multiple clauses of a similar length are used one after the other). *Isocolon* is an excellent structural feature that emphasises hypnotic rhythms that are more likely to lull an audience into indoctrination. If you remember, we also looked at an *isocolon* in in Jamuqa's declaration of allegiance to Chinggis Khan when he said:

> I have ridden my swift grey [horse],
>
> I have put on my leather-thonged armour,
>
> I have grasped my hilted sword,
>
> I have set my notched arrow [against the string],
>
> Let us battle to the death against the Uduyit-Merkits

Both Jamuqa and Goebbels used *isocolon* to create a rhythm in a war speech.

Goebbels used a lot of *argumentum ad populum* in his speeches. *Argumentum ad populum* is a common rhetorical choice for tyrants. In this context, it is an argument that implies that something is true based on the support it receives from the masses. By saying this, Goebbels was reminding his audience that the regime was supported by the people (an important reminder if you want the people in the room to follow you). Truth has no relevance when using *argumentum ad populum*. If the Nazis didn't have the general support of the masses, but they went around convincing enough audiences that they did, eventually a significant enough number of people would believe them to fool the rest. In this instance, a lie repeated can become a truth (this is an abbreviation of a quote which is commonly, and probably apocryphally, attributed to Goebbels).

The final point to focus on in this extract was Goebbels' use of *kairos*: invoking the power of time. This can be seen when he said, 'Everyone must do his duty in this grave hour'. The reference to the hour being grave is a reminder to the audience of the importance and significance of the moment.

In his *Total War* speech, Goebbels used *kairos* no fewer than 51 times. On average, every two minutes or so, Goebbels used a term such as 'today', 'now', or 'this grave hour'. Like Attila the Hun, Chinggis Khan, Mary I, and Napoleon, Goebbels used *kairos* to add momentousness to what he was saying. But he didn't want to add only momentousness. He also wanted to add urgency. Urgency which motivated action.

Kairos adds a sense of importance and urgency which denies people the time to think or scrutinise a message. If a dictatorial leader wants someone to die for their country, they don't say 'tomorrow there is the hypothetical chance that some of you may have to die for your country's honour'; they say, 'now is the time to fight to the death'.

Argumentum ad Hominem and the Vilification of the Jewish People

One of the greatest abuses of rhetoric committed by the Nazi regime was the vilification of the Jewish people. From promoting international conspiracy theories of Jewish control to attempts to dehumanise Jewish people to justify their persecution, the Nazis said whatever they could to scapegoat the Jews for everything that they perceived to be wrong with society and the wider world.

The French philosopher Jean-Paul Sartre once said, 'if the Jew did not exist, the anti-Semite would invent him'. Nazi propaganda, from its speeches to its poisonous literature for young children, took whatever people did not like about the world, and ruthlessly blamed it on 'the Jew': If people did not like disease, they blamed 'the Jew'; If people did not like poverty, they blamed 'the Jew'; If people's children mysteriously disappeared, they blamed 'the Jew'. There is little that 'the Jew' – this hatefully crafted social construct – was not blamed for. And this made real Jews pay for a calculated and premeditated hatred.

Hitler and other leading party figures managed to indoctrinate the German people into hating their Jewish neighbours, with whom they had lived side by side for generations.

In the *Total War* speech, Goebbels said:

> International Jewry is the devilish ferment of decomposition that finds cynical satisfaction in plunging the world into the deepest chaos and destroying ancient cultures that it played no role in building.

By claiming the Jews had no role in creating the 'ancient culture' but were responsible for plunging it into chaos, Goebbels presented the Jewish people as outsiders who, not only did not belong in society, but were also destroying it. To further vilify the Jews, Goebbels not only said that they decayed the ancient cultures of the world, but that they did so with 'cynical satisfaction'. This accusation suggested that international Jews not only harmed society, but they did so intentionally and with malicious intent; thus, turning the false binary into a powerplay – a powerplay that the audience would not want to lose. This sort of language would have appealed to any member of the audience who placed value in their national culture and felt that it was diminishing due to living alongside people from different cultures. Goebbels also invoked Christian imagery through the use of the adjective 'devilish'. Religious language – invoking hell, devils, demons, and such – is often made into a tool for hate.

In the audio recording of the speech, you can hear the monstrous roars of approval and clapping of the German audience whenever Goebbels repeats one of the fabricated accusations against the Jews.

On one occasion in the speech, when Goebbels was talking about how the Jews 'put their host peoples to sleep, paralyzing their defensive abilities' the audience can be heard shouting 'we have experienced it'.

When a speaker is faced with a hyper-responsive audience, they tend to use more forms of structural repetition (such as the *tricolon*) to build the audience into a state of applause. Why does the *tricolon* lead to applause? It is because tricolons build up to a climax which allows the speaker a natural place to pause, which then signals to the audience to clap. An example of a hateful *tricolon* can be seen when Goebbels said:

> Jewry once again reveals itself as the incarnation of evil, as the plastic demon of decay, and the bearer of an international culture-destroying chaos.

After having said this, Goebbels once more received tremendous applause from his audience of 14,000 Nazis.

Sometimes Goebbels used *tricolons*, sometimes he used hyperbolic poetic-sounding language filled with demonic imagery, and sometimes he just used short simple sentences: such as when he said: 'Jewry is a contagious infection'.

Through their words of hate, the Nazis caused an entire people to turn a blind eye to – and, in many cases, actively carry out – the worst persecution and genocide in human history.

The Speech's Ending

After having fired up his audience with *pathos*, added momentousness with *kairos*, and spread hate with *argumentum ad hominem*, the audience were on the brink of exploding with hate, pride, and a thirst for revenge. That is when Goebbels finished his speech with his call to action:

> The nation is ready for anything. The Führer has commanded, and we will follow him. In this hour of national reflection and contemplation, we believe firmly and unshakably in victory. We see it before us, we need only reach for it. We must resolve to subordinate everything to it. That is the duty of the hour. Let the slogan be:
>
> Now, people rise up and let the storm break loose!

Reports suggest that after having delivered this speech, Goebbels boasted that had he instructed the audience to jump off the roof of the building [to their deaths], they would have done it. He believed that he had complete control over the minds of his audience. He probably had achieved that.

This chapter has merely brushed the rhetorical surface of this landmark speech. Despite being one of the most famous Goebbels ever gave, it is just one of thousands delivered by senior Nazi officials during their decades in politics.

The most dramatic speeches of World War Two, the ones which made the biggest impacts and indoctrinated the greatest numbers of people, were not delivered by Goebbels. They were delivered by the Chancellor of Germany, Adolf Hitler: the man who fostered one of the most powerful personality cults of our age.

Adolf Hitler (1889-1945).
Official portrait taken in 1938 by Heinrich Hoffmann.

10.
ADOLF HITLER

Most people already know of the evils committed by Adolf Hitler. They also know of his thundering speeches and his enraptured audiences. But not many people know what he *actually* said. So, what did he say? Why did he say it? And how did he get away with it? The last of these questions highlights the uncomfortable balance between rhetoric and ethics.

During his political career, Hitler gave more than 1,500 speeches. It would be impractical in a single book, let alone a single chapter, to give an accurate summary of what he said, why he said it, and how he got away with it. Instead, I will focus on two topics, which can give a sense of the content and style of his discourse.

The Rise to Power

Like Napoleon, Adolf Hitler took control of a nation he wasn't a native of. He was born into a modest family in Austria-Hungary (modern-day Austria) on 20 April 1889. As a teenager, he argued with his parents and would slap his mother when they had disagreements. His father died in 1903. In 1907, using charity money for orphans, Hitler moved to Vienna to study art but was rejected from art schools. When he was 18 years old, his mother died from breast cancer and he ended up living in a homeless shelter working as a labourer – desperately trying to sell his watercolour paintings for money. In 1914, he moved to Munich and, when World War One broke out, he volunteered to serve in the army.

During the war, he was decorated for bravery twice, receiving the Iron Cross first and second class. He was briefly blinded by mustard gas but made a full recovery. After the World War One, Hitler began to engage in politics, later writing that Germany's defeat and humiliation prompted him to want to 'liberate' Germany and make it 'great'. His first recorded antisemitic comments were in a letter he wrote in 1919, in which he suggested that all Jews should leave German lands. At the time, both Austria-Hungary and Germany were deeply antisemitic places and Hitler would have encountered antisemitism in cartoons, in pamphlets, in cinemas as well as in conversations he had with the people around him.

Hitler worked in politics full time from 1920 and began giving passionate speeches against the Jews at around the same time. As his popularity grew, so too did the numbers of his supporters. They became known as the Brownshirts and, similarly to Mussolini's Blackshirts, they terrorised people in society who advocated for different politics as well as anyone who was Jewish.

Eventually, in 1923, they caused so much trouble that Adolf Hitler was arrested for treason and imprisoned. He was incarcerated for one year, and it was during this time that he wrote *Mein Kampf* ('My Struggle').

After his release from prison, Hitler's popularity soared. As Germany's economic and social problems mounted, people connected more and more with his aggressive style of communication. He would shout in his speeches, shake his fists, and use an abundance of racist tropes as he raged about the injustices he claimed had been committed against the German people. He was seen by some as a radical, and attempts were made to ban him from speaking in public.

Following a series of electoral victories for the Nazi party, Hitler was appointed Chancellor on 30 January 1933. In power, Hitler began dismantling the democratic institutions and centralising power around himself. Shortly after his election, on 27 February 1933, the German parliament building (The Reichstag) burnt down in an apparent arson attack. This was blamed on communists and Hitler argued that the only effective solution was to grant himself emergency powers. There was political opposition to this, but Hitler's paratroopers intimidated politicians into voting in favour of the Enabling Act of 1933, which granted him power to rule by decree without any input from the Weimar or the Reichstag (the two main bodies of German democracy). Hitler had become the undisputed master of Germany.

Once in power, he started sending his political opponents to concentration camps. He also began introducing a series of laws to oppress and bully the Jewish communities of Germany, and started to expand Germany's borders.

The Destruction of the Jewish Race in Europe

One of Hitler's key political demands throughout his career was creating *Lebensraum* (meaning 'room to live') for the German people. His policies advocated removing from society anyone who was deemed to be different. This idea of space being limited, and being exclusive, was prominent in his rhetoric and his attempts to manipulate the masses. Specifically, he wanted to clear out the Jewish people in Europe so that there would be more space – and, according to him, healthier space – for the German people. Germans angered by the economic and social suffering of the post-World War One economy supported him. As he enraged them more, his support grew.

Through his speeches, Hitler incited such hatred, that people in Germany were willing to participate in, or turn a blind eye to, what is considered by many to be the greatest atrocity in human history – a genocide that murdered more than 6 million Jews.

Hitler believed that an effective message needed to be repeated in a speech in simple terms, again, and again, and again. That is why senior Nazis scapegoated the Jewish people in countless speeches.

The extract which I will use for this chapter was chosen as an example of antisemitism in Hitler's speeches by Yad Vashem (The World Holocaust Remembrance Centre). The speech was given in the Reichstag (the German parliament building) on 30 January 1939. Hitler began his tirade by saying:

> ...In connection with the Jewish question I have this to say: it is a shameful spectacle to see how the whole democratic world is oozing sympathy for the poor tormented Jewish people, but remains hard-hearted and obdurate when it comes to helping them which is surely, in view of its attitude, an obvious duty. The arguments that are brought up as an excuse for not helping them actually speak for us Germans and Italians.

Hitler used vicious sarcasm when he referred to the 'poor tormented Jewish people'. He used this sarcasm as part of his criticism of what he referred to as 'the whole democratic world' (by which, he was referring to his enemies). By having attempted to prove an inconsistency in international attitudes towards Jews, Hitler used a rhetorical feature called *argumentum ad rem*. *Argumentum ad rem* is when a speaker attempts to criticise the logic of an opponent's argument. In rhetorical terms, *argumentum ad rem* is an attack on *logos*.

As well as being *argumentum ad rem*, this extract is also *argumentum ad hominem* (vilifying an opponent) – this is because Hitler used the flawed logic with the intention of suggesting to his audience the character flaws of the other nations – and, obviously, also against the Jews.

In simple terms, Hitler stated: *how can the world criticise how we treat the Jewish people when they don't do anything to help them either?* By raising this point, Hitler not only vilified the international community, but also cast allusions on the Jewish people. While in this instance he merely questioned the popularity of the Jewish people, he was more explicit about it later on in the same speech; making the *argumentum ad hominem* more explicit.

Hitler used statistics (a common form of *logos*) to imply that it was impractical and unfair for Germany to have Jews, based on the density of its population. He said:

> For this is what they [the other nations] say, 'We are not in a position to take in the Jews.' Yet in these empires there are not 10 people to the square kilometre. While Germany, with her 135 inhabitants to the square kilometre, is supposed to have room for them!

With only the mildest critical thinking, it is apparent that these figures can't be trusted. First of all, comparing the population density of Nazi

Germany with the US will produce wildly misleading results – for several reasons. One is that the US includes well over one million square kilometres of uninhabitable desert. At the time, probably unknown to Hitler's audience, comparable countries actually had even more people in the same amount of space than Germany's 135 inhabitants per square kilometre. Britain's population density at the time was around 188 people per km sq, Japan's was approximately 191, and the Netherlands' was 212. The population of New York City in 1943 was 10,549 people per square kilometre. Hitler used a statistic that sounded shocking; however, in context, it did not really mean anything significant. This example is symbolic of the power of dishonest *logos* and how it can manipulate reasoning and ethics.

(Hitler's argument of space also ignored the attachment the Jewish people would have had to their homes, land and neighbourhoods. Tyrants often speak as if populations can just be moved without much effort or emotional turmoil).

Hitler then went on to use the common metaphor of referring to Jews as a disease. He said:

> For hundreds of years Germany was good enough to receive these elements, although they possessed nothing except infectious political and physical diseases. What they possess today, they have by a very large extent gained at the cost of the less astute German nation by the most reprehensible manipulations.

Opening with a reference to time (*kairos*), Hitler drew his audience's attention to the amount of time Germany had been receiving Jews. He then spoke about the 'political and physical diseases' that they had brought with them. Tyrants and dictators often attack the hygiene of outsiders they want to vilify as a form of *argumentum ad hominem*. Hitler emphasised this age-old trope with the *antithesis* of 'political and physical' which allowed his audience to attach themselves to the one that emotionally resonated most strongly with them.

Hitler continued his vilification by suggesting that whatever Jews had achieved they had achieved through 'reprehensible manipulations'. His reason for saying this would have probably been to negate any sympathy that his audience might have had towards Jewish people. For example, if a member of the audience had a Jewish neighbour who was polite, clean, and friendly, they might think Hitler was wrong. By saying that their achievements were the results of manipulation, Hitler suggested that the 'good Jews' were only so because of cultural or monetary theft. This is another antisemitic trope common in other forms of othering used by extremists.

Hitler went on:

> Today we are merely paying this people what it deserves. When the German nation was, thanks to the inflation instigated and carried through by Jews, deprived of the entire savings which it had accumulated in years of honest work, when the rest of the world took away the German nation's foreign investments, when we were divested of the whole of our colonial possessions, these philanthropic considerations evidently carried little noticeable weight with democratic statesmen.

In this, Hitler blamed most of Germany's most serious problems – the economic, political, and social problem – on the Jewish people. This is one of thousands of examples of Hitler using conspiracy theories and misinformation to vilify the Jews as a common enemy and thus unite the 'German' people. To further emphasise how much damage the Jews had supposedly done to Germany, Hitler used a *tricolon of anaphora* (repetition at the start of a clause, sentence or paragraph) with his three clauses beginning with 'when'.

The next part of Hitler's ranting speech went on to list the injustices done to the German people:

> After more than 800,000 children of the nation had died of hunger and undernourishment at the close of the War, we witnessed almost one million milking cows being driven away from us in accordance with the cruel paragraphs of a dictate which the humane democratic apostles of the world forced upon us as a peace treaty. We witnessed over one million German prisoners of war being retained in confinement for no reason at all for a whole year after the War was ended. We witnessed over one and a half million Germans being torn away from all that they possessed in the territories lying on our frontiers, and being whipped out with practically only what they wore on their backs. We had to endure having millions of our fellow countrymen torn from us without their consent, and without their being afforded the slightest possibility of existence. I could supplement these examples with dozens of the most cruel kind. For this reason, we ask to be spared all sentimental talk.

The first thing to note is Hitler's emotive language. Hitler used *pathos* (words aimed at stirring emotion) to elicit a range of emotions from his audience: sadness, grief, anger and revenge, to name but a few. Hitler emphasised the scale of the injustice by the *anaphoric tricolon* of 'We witnessed'. For each of these clauses, he also said 'one million'. Hitler broke the tricolon of *anaphora* by saying: 'We had to endure...' This breaking of the pattern of repetition might be seen as a use of another technique, *hyperbaton* (when a structure is broken, or word order is inverted, to create emphasis).

After hyping up the audience's emotions – a common tactic to get people to stop scrutinising arguments as clearly as they otherwise might – Hitler went on to use the common populist language of independence. He said:

> The German nation does not wish its interests to be determined and controlled by any foreign nation. France to the French, England to the English, America to the Americans, and Germany to the Germans. We are resolved to prevent the settlement in our country of a strange people which was capable of snatching for itself all the leading positions in the land, and to oust it. Above all, German culture, as its name alone shows, is German and not Jewish.

Hitler used the repetition of clauses of a similar length when he said: 'France to the French, England to the English, America to the Americans, and Germany to the Germans'. The rhythmic beating of this *isocolon* (clauses of a similar length) would have impassioned his audience with every repetition. In these cases, a speaker usually says something that the audience understands. Then they toy with the audience's emotions by repeating the same sentiment with a different example. And, finally, they climax with a powerful declaration that closes their argument – which, in this case, was: 'Germany to the Germans'. In the context of this speech: not for the Jews.

A few paragraphs later, Hitler went on to say:

> The world has sufficient space for settlements, but we must once and for all get rid of the opinion that the Jewish race was only

> created by God for the purpose of being in a certain percentage a parasite living on the body and the productive work of other nations. The Jewish race will have to adapt itself to sound constructive activity as other nations do, or sooner or later it will succumb to a crisis of an inconceivable magnitude.

Nazi rhetoric often referred to Jews as parasites. Using metaphors to dehumanise groups of people in this way is a common tool in the rhetoric of tyranny, and depicting Jews as parasites is a common antisemitic trope that has existed ever since the Romans banished the Jews from their homeland. In many cases, Jews were refused work, and were then criticised for being poor. And if a Jew was not poor, they were criticised for being rich. As is the case for most forms of racism, antisemitism contains logical fallacies and inconsistencies which are openly accepted by those who seek to spread hatred.

The most famous part of this speech is its conclusion. It is where Hitler dramatically spoke of his 'prophecies', threatened the Jews with 'annihilation', and called on the people of the world to unite against their 'common enemy'. The extract ends with the following words:

> In the course of my life, I have very often been a prophet, and have usually been ridiculed for it. During the time of my struggle for power it was in the first instance the Jewish race which only received my prophecies with laughter when I said that I would one day take over the leadership of the State, and with it that of the whole nation, and that I would then among many other things settle the Jewish problem. Their laughter was uproarious, but I think that for some time now they have been laughing on the other side of their face. Today I will once more be a prophet: If the international Jewish financiers in and outside Europe should succeed in plunging the nations

once more into a world war, then the result will not be the Bolshevization of the earth, and thus the victory of Jewry, but the annihilation of the Jewish race in Europe!

...The nations are no longer willing to die on the battlefield so that this unstable international race may profiteer from a war or satisfy its Old Testament vengeance. The Jewish watchword 'Workers of the world unite' will be conquered by a higher realization, namely 'Workers of all classes and of all nations, recognize your common enemy!'

In this dramatic ending, Hitler accused the 'Jewish financiers' of the world for causing World War One. Simply using the term 'Jewish financiers' is a dog whistle to a longstanding antisemitic trope of Jewish usury – a trope which is excellently deconstructed and rebuked in Julie Mell's book *The Myth of the Medieval Jewish Moneylender*. Hitler also called the Jews an 'international race', talked about their 'Old Testament vengeance', and ended by calling them the 'common enemy'.

Adolf Hitler closed the speech with a hypothetical slogan, which was an imperative – a command. As we saw from Goebbels and many other examples, imperative sentences are powerful tools for closing hateful speeches. In this case, it ('recognise your common enemy') is a call to action, a warning, and a forewarning of future atrocities yet to be committed.

January 1941

Two years later, in January 1941, Hitler gave a similar speech where he again blamed Jews for all of Germany's problems, and characterised them as having influence over Germany's enemies. About England, he said:

> And yet to speak today of England's World Power or of England as the master of the world, is nothing but an illusion. To begin with her internal situation: England, in spite of her world conquests is perhaps socially the most backward State in Europe. Socially backward-that is, a State orientated entirely in the interests of a comparatively small and thin upper stratum and the Jewish clique with which it is allied.

Throughout this speech, and in many others, Hitler spoke of the 'Jewish clique' as a form of *argumentum ad hominem*. The idea of a 'clique' reinforced the narrative of Jews being self-serving to the detriment of the nation they were living in.

But the *argumentum ad hominem* was also directed towards England, which at the time was still considered a superpower. By suggesting that England had 'orientated entirely' to the 'Jewish clique', Hitler insulted England on two counts: first, he suggested that its strength was an illusion; second, he got his audience to associate England with Jewish control.

Later in the same speech, Hitler said:

> This collection of capitalist interests on the one hand, Jewish instincts of hatred and the emigrants' lust for revenge, succeeded in increasingly beclouding the world, enveloping it in phrases, and in inciting it against the present German Reich, just as against the Reich which preceded us. At that time they opposed the Germany of the Kaiser, this time they opposed National-Socialist Germany. In fact, they opposed any Germany which might be in existence.

Presenting Jews as disgruntled and vengeful is an historic antisemitic trope. Shylock, the Jewish merchant in Shakespeare's *The Merchant of Venice* asks: 'If you wrong us, shall we not revenge?' The same characteristics were projected onto the Jews by the Nazis, which is demonstrated by Hitler speaking of their 'lust for revenge' in this extract.

His vilification continues to echo the rhetoric of his past speech by suggesting that Germany's Jews hated Germany. Hitler suggested that if the world fell into another world war it would be both the fault and the end of the Jews. He said:

> I do not want to miss pointing out what I pointed out on 3rd of September [1940] in the German Reichstag, that if Jewry were to plunge the world into war, the role of Jewry would be finished in Europe. They may laugh about it today, as they laughed before about my prophecies. The coming months and years will prove that I prophesied rightly in this case too. But we can see already how our racial peoples which are today still hostile to us will one day recognise the greater inner enemy, and that they too will then enter with us into a great common front. The front of Aryan mankind against Jewish-International exploitation and destruction of nations.

These examples are just extracts of two speeches given by Hitler between when he entered politics in 1919 and when he died in 1945 – he gave 1,523 more. They hopefully showcase, however, the multifaceted depths and complexities of Hitler's rhetoric. In this oration, as in many of his other speeches, Hitler appealed to his audiences' emotions, whipped them up into a frenzy, and unleashed it on the Jewish people: a people who were wholly innocent of the crimes of which they were accused.

Hitler and the Nazis show us the true terror of rhetoric and the spoken word. They show us how its abuse can lead to genocide. They show us how the minds of the masses – teachers, doctors, cobblers, seamstresses – can be overpowered with fear and hate, how they can be twisted in malice. And were.

Rhetoric does have an evil side. This is it.

Joseph Stalin (1878-1953).
Stalin at the Tehran Conference, 1943.

11.
JOSEPH STALIN

A man named Ioseb Besarionis dze Jughashvili was born in the winter of 1878 in the Russian Empire to an impoverished family. His father was an alcoholic cobbler, and his mother a washerwoman. Despite his humble origins, Ioseb Besarionis dze Jughashvili would go on to become one of the most powerful and violent men the world had ever known. It was in 1912 that he started writing articles under his new pseudonym: Stalin.

The word 'Stalin' means 'Man of Steel'. Before he took power the man was vaunting his ethos: hard, cold, and ruthless. It would follow that his speeches would emulate those qualities. His time would soon come.

In 1917, Russia fell into civil war. The tyrannical monarch, Tsar Nicholas II and his family, were deposed and brutally executed in 1918. In 1922, the new Communist regime headed by Vladimir Lenin founded the Union of Soviet Socialist Republics (USSR)[1]. Lenin's right-hand man was Joseph Stalin.

After Lenin suffered his first stroke in 1922 and began to deteriorate, Stalin consolidated his power. When Lenin eventually died in 1924, Stalin grabbed as much power as he could and destroyed anyone who was seen as an obstacle: in some cases this was figurative but in others literal. During his reign, he introduced the idea of collective farming which was a leading cause of a devastating famine which killed millions through starvation.

During the Second World War, Stalin's USSR was at war with Germany. His own son, Yakov Dzhugashvili, died in a Nazi concentration camp after Stalin refused to have him released in a prisoner exchange. There is some historical contention regarding how Yakov was captured and how he died, but his father's ruthless rejection of a prisoner swap is well documented.

Despite initially losing huge amounts of land to Nazi Germany, the USSR eventually managed to begin reclaiming territory after territory. This happened around the time of its great victory over Germany's Nazi forces at the Battle of Stalingrad.

Stalin's Speeches

While Goebbels, Hitler and other senior Nazi figures were spreading their speeches of hate, Stalin was propagating his own. Soviet rhetoric does not have the same reputation as that of the Nazis, perhaps because the cold Soviet *ethos* was more stoical than the flamboyant Nazi approach to language.

---

[1] Territories: Russia, Estonia, Latvia, Lithuania, Belarus, Ukraine, Moldova, Georgia, Armenia, Azerbaijan, Kazakhstan, Uzbekistan, Turkmenistan, Kyrgyzstan, and Tajikistan.

Nevertheless, Stalin gave thumping speeches, often war speeches calling for the death and destruction of the German regime. One such speech was delivered at the Red Army Parade on the Red Square on 7 November 1941.

Towards the opening of this speech, Stalin said:

> Comrades, it is in strenuous circumstances that we are today celebrating the 24th anniversary of the October Revolution. The perfidious attack of the German brigands and the war which has been forced upon us have placed our country in jeopardy. We have temporarily lost a number of regions, the enemy has appeared at the gates of Leningrad and Moscow.

Stalin's use of 'Comrades' to address the audience was a common feature in communist rhetoric. It insinuated equality between the speaker and audience. The use of such an egalitarian address was a form of ethos that worked to build on the proud bond of the leadership and the masses: a bond which communists held dear.

Stalin went on to use *kairos* when he spoke about the momentousness of the time in which he was speaking. As well as explicitly using the word 'today', Stalin spoke about it being 24 years since the anniversary of the October revolution. There is little doubt that his audience were aware that that particular day was the 24th anniversary of an important event; nevertheless, by specifically stating it, Stalin gave them time to reflect on its significance: an emotive significance.

Importantly, Stalin conceded they were celebrating in 'strenuous circumstances'. This is a rhetorical feature called *concessio*. *Concessio* is when a speaker acknowledges a disadvantage or a point which supports the other side's argument. This concession was then emphasised later in the speech when Stalin spoke of the country being in 'jeopardy' and how the USSR had 'temporarily lost a number of regions' and that the enemy had 'appeared at the gates of Leningrad and Moscow'.

One may wonder why a leader would show such vulnerability by strengthening an opponent's image. However, leaders will often boost the image of their opponents to make themselves seem even greater for overpowering them. Imagine that David was gloating after he killed Goliath. Would he have played down Goliath's size or exaggerated it? Stalin spoke about Germany's success and might in one sentence only to trumpet its domination by the USSR's in the next, just as Emperor Wu Zetian had similarly praised the rebels she had defeated in battle.

Stalin went on to say:

> The enemy reckoned that after the very first blow our army would be dispersed, and our country would be forced to its knees. But the enemy sadly miscalculated. In spite of the temporary reverses our army and navy are heroically repulsing the enemy's attacks along the whole front and inflicting heavy losses upon him, while our country – our entire country – has formed itself into one fighting camp in order, together with our Army and our Navy, to encompass the defeat of the German invaders.

In this message of heroic victory, Stalin presented the entire country as a united force. The repetition of 'our country – our entire country' emphasised that unity. This apparent hesitation and correction can be seen as a use of *aporia*. *Aporia* is a rhetorical feature where a speaker appears to hesitate and correct themselves to give the impression of spontaneity and thus authenticity.

More importantly, in this response to his own use of *concessio*, Stalin presented the country as a 'fighting camp'. This metaphor was used to motivate his people to keep on fighting. By praising what he wanted to see more of, Stalin was subliminally telling the people what they needed to be. During wartime, it is important to keep morale high in victory as well as defeat.

Stalin also used *argumentum ad hominem* when he vilified the German *ethos* by calling them 'invaders' and 'brigands'. These signifiers were, arguably, a dismissive oversimplification of Germany's military power, which would have gone down well with an audience who hoped that it was beatable.

Towards the end of that speech, Stalin readdressed his audience. In a way, this can be seen as a use of *apostrophe*, similar to that we saw in Napoleon's proclamation (when he addressed the quartermaster-general), although Stalin addressed the individual groups within his audience rather than someone special to reprimand troops. Speakers often list the groups who make up their audiences as a way of making them feel seen, understood, and valued.

Stalin said:

> Comrades, men of the Red Army and Red Navy, commanders and political instructors, men and women guerrillas, the whole world is looking towards you as a force capable of destroying the plundering hordes of German robbers. The enslaved peoples of Europe who have fallen beneath the yoke of the German robbers look towards you as their liberators. A great liberating mission has fallen to your lot. Be worthy of that mission! The war you are waging is a war of liberation, a just war. Let the heroic images of our great forefathers – Alexander Nevsky, Dmitry Donskoy, Kuzma Minin, Dmitry Pozharsky, Aleksandr

> Suvorov and Mikhail Kutuzov – inspire you in this war! May the victorious banner of the great Lenin be your lodestar!
>
> Fight until the German invaders are utterly smashed!
>
> Death to the German invaders!
>
> Long live our glorious country, her liberty and her independence!
>
> Forward to glory under the banner of Lenin!

After addressing the groups within his audience, Stalin sought to instil pride. When Stalin said 'the whole world is looking towards you as a force capable of destroying the plundering hordes of German robbers', not only was he saying the USSR could win the war, he was saying that it would have international glory when it did so. Stalin then repeated the idea of the audience being watched when, in the next sentence, he said: 'The enslaved peoples of Europe who have fallen beneath the yoke of the German robbers look towards you as their liberators'. The audience's mission was much more serious than merely repelling the invaders: Russia must save the enslaved peoples of the whole of Europe! In this second repetition of being watched, Stalin referenced the moral imperative to stop Germany: an imperative that would have sat well with his audience.

As well as referencing a moral imperative, Stalin also peppered his speech with actual imperatives. He literally told his audience what to do. The repetition of commands began when he said: 'A great liberating mission has fallen to your lot. Be worthy of that mission!' He went on to order them to 'fight' and 'go forwards'. These imperative verbs were all rhetorically loaded to elicit an emotional response from the USSR's citizens, from the soldiers to the labourers.

In his reference to the 'great forefathers', Stalin invoked – whilst simultaneously shaping – the *ethos* of the Russian people. He listed national heroes throughout history whom his audience would have known. Russians would have grown up hearing tales of their glory. Invoking historical figures in this way can be seen as a further emphasis of *kairos*, highlighting that this moment is a moment of glory as the tales of old.

It is interesting to note that Stalin's reference to the 'great forefathers' is similar to Queen Ranavalona I's mention of the 'tombs of the Vazimba'. Both Stalin and Ranavalona I wanted to remind their audience of their glorious heritage.

Similarly to how Goebbels employed short punchy sentences to emphasise key moments of his speeches, so too did Stalin when addressing his final battle cry ('Death to the German invaders') to his stoic audience. The short sentences were further emphasised by the exclamations in the published transcript. Each point would have led to strong and rapturous agreement.

It is clear to see from this speech that Stalin used exactly the same methods as previous dictators to galvanise his audience. Now, this speech was given in a time of struggle. We will now fast forward four and a half years to look at a speech that Stalin gave in a time of victory: specifically, 9 May 1945, by which time Hitler was dead and Germany had surrendered.

Stalin gave an important radio address to the peoples of the USSR. He opened his speech with a dramatic proclamation:

COMRADES! Men and women compatriots!

The great day of victory over Germany has come. Fascist Germany, forced to her knees by the Red Army and the troops of our Allies, has acknowledged herself defeated and declared unconditional surrender.

Stalin again used the personification of a nation being brought to its knees, the same thing he claimed Germany had tried to do to Russia.

Similarly to the 1941 speech, Stalin again opened with *kairos* to emphasise the time in which he was speaking: this was, after all, an important moment. The *kairos* was further emphasised when he said later:

> Now we can state with full justification that the historic day of the final defeat of Germany, the day of the great victory of our people over German imperialism has come.

Note the *anaphoric* repetition of 'day,' which emphasises *kairos*. The objective of this speech was to share the glory and motivate people to further support his rule. The more he could hype up this victory, the greater was his claim to power. But even the most arrogant tyrant cannot celebrate such a costly victory, which would have been known to everyone in the audience, without mentioning the losses. Stalin went on to say:

> The great sacrifices we made in the name of the freedom and independence of our Motherland, the incalculable privations and sufferings experienced by our people in the course of the war, the intense work in the rear and at the front, placed on the altar of the Motherland, have not been in vain, and have been crowned by complete victory over the enemy. The age-long struggle of the Slav peoples for their existence and their independence has ended in victory over the German invaders and German tyranny.

Here Stalin used a *tricolon* ('great sacrifices', 'incalculable privations', and 'intense work'), which he claimed had 'not been in vain'. Ultimately, this is a form of *logos*, as Stalin made the logical argument that the outcome was worth the loss.

The triadic repetition to emphasise the cost was emphasised with a number of other rhetorical features. For example, he used *antithesis* when he mentioned 'the intense work in the rear and at the front'; he used *epistrophe* when he repeated 'Motherland' at the end of two of the three clauses; he used *abundantia* when he spoke of 'freedom and independence'. All of this rhetorical repetition was used to emphasise the scale of the suffering in order to magnify the size of the victory.

Stalin again returned to *kairos* when he spoke of the 'age-long struggle' before moving onto the *anaphoric* repetition of 'the German invaders and Germany tyranny' as a form of *argumentum ad hominem*.

After this vilification of Germany, Stalin then made it personal by directing his *argumentum ad hominem* against Hitler as an individual. He said:

> Hitler's crazy ideas were not fated to come true – the progress of the war scattered them to the winds. In actual fact the direct opposite of the Hitlerites' ravings has taken place. Germany is utterly defeated. The German troops are surrendering. The Soviet Union is celebrating Victory, although it does not intend either to dismember or to destroy Germany.

As well as ridiculing Hitler, Stalin used another *tricolon* to again emphasise the Soviet victory. It is interesting that Stalin chose not to talk of the destruction of Germany, only the destruction of the 'German invaders'. He even made a point of specifying that the USSR would not destroy or dismember Germany – perhaps hinting at moral superiority or trying to avoid dangerous political insinuations.

Stalin ended his glorious victory speech by saying:

> Comrades! The Great Patriotic War has ended in our complete victory. The period of war in Europe is over. The period of peaceful development has begun.
>
> I congratulate you upon victory, my dear men and women compatriots!
>
> Glory to our heroic Red Army, which upheld the independence of our Motherland and won victory over the enemy!
>
> Glory to our great people, the people victorious!
>
> Eternal glory to the heroes who fell in the struggle against the enemy and gave their lives for the freedom and happiness of our people!

Similarly to his speech in 1941, Stalin finished with a series of rousing exclamations.

Towards the end of the war, and throughout the rest of his reign, Joseph Stalin's health was on the decline. He died in March 1953 in Kuntsevo Dacha, his private residence. Throughout his reign, Stalin, the cobbler's son, is thought to have been responsible for millions of deaths: nearly a million were executed, and millions more died from forced labour, deportation, and famine. Figures are hard to calculate, but some estimates hold Stalin responsible for the deaths of more than 20 million people.

Joseph Stalin

Eva Péron (1919-1952).
Photograph taken by Pinélides Aristóbulo Fusco in 1948.

12.
EVA PERÓN

Even though Juan Perón was a Nazi-sympathising paedophilic demagogue, Peronism – the political movement named in his honour – is still popular in Argentina, represented by the Justicialist Party which has a membership of nearly 4 million. Juan and his wife Eva (Evita) Perón are still considered icons by many people across the world. So much so that Eva Perón is still on the Argentine 100 pesos banknote. It is worth noting that Peronism is a complicated and, at times, shifting movement. Even today, it means many different things to many different people and views on the movement can be polarising.

Juan Perón, a man with Sardinian heritage, supposedly took inspiration from Mussolini, the founding father of facism. His presidency echoed the style and character of a number of fascist governments of the time – authoritarian rule, populist rhetoric, and a cult leader who was expected to be worshipped at any expense. Government power was wielded ruthlessly, and the Argentine media was kept on a short leash. Despite the great popularity of Perónism and its leading couple, Juan and Eva oversaw a tyrannical regime which, while it may have strongly represented the values of many working-class Argentines, was morally corrupt, nepotistic, and dangerous.

Under Perón, Argentina gave sanctuary to senior Nazi war criminals such as Joseph Mengele and Adolf Eichmann. Mengele, one of the most notorious historical figures from Nazi Germany, was a scientist who conducted inhumane and murderous experiments on Jewish prisoners (especially twins and children). Eichmann was one of the organisers of the Holocaust. Not only did Perón's government harbour such people, but it also actively encouraged them to emigrate and welcomed them with open arms. Why? Because even though they were fully aware of the atrocities committed by the Nazis, they were keen to share in the stolen treasures which accompanied their naturalisation.

Colonel Juan Perón was a military figure who played a significant role in a coup in 1943 which overthrew and replaced the civilian government with a military one. Not wanting a major political role, Juan accepted the position of Secretary of Labour and Social Welfare. Not long after, in 1944, he met Eva, who had had a hard start in life. While she was a young child, Eva's father abandoned the family, leaving her and her mother to live in poverty as social outcasts. At the age of 15, in 1934, Eva left her poverty-stricken background with a boyfriend to go to Buenos Aires. The relationship didn't last but it was in Buenos Aires that Eva began her career in performance, acting, and modelling. As her beauty and talent brought her fame, she began meeting increasingly important people, including the rising politician Juan Perón.

Juan Perón became Minister for War, and then Vice President. In early October 1945, however, Perón was ousted from government and placed under arrest by a rival Argentine military group. After mass protests, he was freed on 17 October – which has been marked every year since as Loyalty Day.

A few days after his release, Juan married Eva. From that moment on, the two of them campaigned ruthlessly and tirelessly to get Juan elected as President. In February 1946, they succeeded. From the moment they married to the moment she died, Eva Perón did everything within her power to promote her husband as a cult leader, whom everyone should be willing to sacrifice their life for. How did she manage to successfully transform Juan into a cult figure? She gave speeches – lots of speeches!

Eva's Speeches

By the end of her life, Eva Perón was a cult figure herself, loved and adored by the masses. However, her popularity wasn't as strong towards the beginning of her time as first lady. Records suggest that her first speech did not go well. She arrived at the venue two hours late, and the audience, who were at this point fed up of standing in the sweltering Argentine heat, booed her to the point that she couldn't be heard. It was a disaster. Within a year, she had learnt the skills needed to be a successful public speaker and was never booed like that again.

One of Eva's most famous speeches was delivered in Buenos Aires on Loyalty Day, 1951. Standing on a balcony, overlooking an audience of tens of thousands of cheering people, shouting into a microphone, Eva gave what was possibly the most momentous speech of her lifetime. By this point, everyone knew that she was dying. She was diagnosed with cervical cancer in 1950, and by the time of this speech her health was quickly deteriorating. Eva said that she had a debt to pay to the people of Argentina. 'It doesn't matter to me if I have to leave a shred of my life along the way in order to repay it,' she said.

Reports suggest that she was so ill during that speech that she had to be drugged up with medication just to keep her standing. Despite this, she gave a truly remarkable speech: a declaration of love to Perón and the people of Argentina. But, more than that, it was a rallying cry to die for Perón and to die for the people of Argentina. She said:

> Nothing I have, nothing I am, nothing I think is mine: it's Perón's. I will not tell you the usual lies: I won't tell you that I don't deserve this. Yes, I deserve this, my general. I deserve it for one thing alone, which is worth more than all the gold in the world: I deserve it for all I've done for the love of this people. I'm not important because of what I've done; I'm not important because of what I've renounced; I'm not important because of what I am or have. I have only one thing that matters, and I have it in my heart. It sets my soul aflame, it wounds my flesh and burns in my sinews: it's love for this people and for Perón.

It is clear from this short extract that Eva understood how to use *anaphoric tricolons* to create tension and mystery for her audience. By repeating the beginning of her clauses three times, she was able to create a powerful rhythm to lull her audience into a frenzy of passion. In this short extract, there are no fewer than four examples of some form of *anaphoric tricolon*. She then combined that rhetorically rhythmic repetition with a strong use of *ethos* and *pathos*, to demonstrate her love for Perón and the people of Argentina.

She opened by attributing everything that she had to offer to her husband. This repetition of 'nothing' is the first *tricolon of anaphora*.

These words were also a clear declaration of *ethos*. She consolidated her values, her beliefs, and her role as a supportive wife.

She continued using *anaphora* with the repetition of 'I will not tell you' – a statement which implied that while others might lie, she was being genuine and authentic. This is a further consolidation of the virtuous *ethos* which she presented to her audience. The pursuit of authenticity is a challenge in public speaking and different speakers approach it in different ways. Some will try and memorise a speech to avoid using notes, others will outright use the unverifiable statement: 'I am not lying'.

Eva used a second *anaphoric tricolon* when she started three sentences with 'I deserve' (technically one starts with 'Yes' but rhetorically still emphasises the 'I deserve' as the opening). By saying that she deserved the recognition and the award, her audience would have instinctively questioned why. The reason Eva made a point of repeatedly saying that she deserved this award was to set her audience up for a grand reveal. She used the classic tactic of saying that she didn't deserve it for the reason they think, but rather for another reason. Mystery often engages a listener to pay attention by creating the suspense of desire.

She went on to further set up this big reveal with a third *tricolon of anaphora* when she repeated, 'I am not important because' – using a sneaky little rhetorical feature we have not encountered before called *occultatio*. *Occultatio* is when a speaker draws an audience's attention to something by casually mentioning that they won't mention it. Eva used this repetition as a form of humble bragging: her use of *occultatio* would have reminded her audience how great she was; thus, further bolstering her *ethos*. All the things that Eva said she was not important for would likely have been, in the minds of the audience, what she was important for. By subverting their expectation, she hooked their attention and expressed what would have likely been projected as authenticity.

To further add to the tension of what this big reveal was, Eva used a third *tricolon of anaphora* when she said: 'It sets my soul aflame, it wounds my flesh and burns in my sinews: it's love for this people and for Perón'. This flowery and poetic reveal was drenched in *pathos*. She used romantic – almost sexual – language: words which are synonymous with burning desire.

This grand declaration of love, this ultimate compliment for the audience, is another example of the rhetorical trick of *comprobatio* (flattery). Eva wanted the audience to adore her, so she adored the audience. Flattery can often be one of the most powerful tools of persuasion.

Eva said:

> I gave you thanks, my general, for having taught me to know and love them. If this people asked me for my life, I would joyfully give it, for the happiness of one descamisado[1] is worth more than my entire life.

At the end of this section, Eva again expressed pathos when she spoke of the joy and happiness of giving her life and dying for the people and for Perón. This oxymoron seems somewhat ironic as it could be

---

1 Descamisado is a positive and, arguably, empowering term for a poor person. The literal translation is 'shirtless' which was originally a derogatory term for the working classes, but later was reclaimed as a term of solidarity and empowerment.

an apt metaphor for the popularity and brutality of Eva and Juan's rule, and perhaps even for Peronism itself.

Later, in the same speech, Eva went on to warn her audience about the enemy. She said:

> The danger has not passed. Every Argentinian worker must keep his eyes open and not fall asleep, for the enemies work in the shade of treason and sometimes are hidden behind a smile or an extended hand.

History has always had the trope of the 'enemy within our midst', a mysterious villain disguised among us. Such enemies are flaunted by tyrants to invoke fear and hatred in their audiences and, by doing so, control the masses. After all, a jumpy and scared audience with a common enemy is easier to indoctrinate than a calm and measured one at peace with everyone and everything. Eva Perón knew this.

The violence in her loving speech then escalated when she called on people to die for the country and for Perón. After declaring her love and warning them of the enemy, Eva said:

> The enemies of the people, of Perón and the Fatherland, have also long known that Perón and Eva Perón are ready to die for this people. Now they also know that the people are ready to die for Perón.
>
> Compañeros[2], I ask just one thing today: that all of us publicly vow to defend Perón and to fight for him until death. And our oath will be shouted for a minute so that our cry can reach the last corner of the earth: Our lives for Perón!

---

2 Compañeros has the same meaning as comrade.

Here Eva used a fancy rhetorical pattern of repetition known as a chiasmus. Chiasmus refers to repetition which follows an A/B/B/A pattern. In this instance that **Perón (A)** is willing to die for the ***people (B)*** and the ***people (B)*** are willing to die for **Perón (A)**. The wonder of a chiasmus is that anything that fits into the A/B/B/A structure automatically sounds more profound than if it was stated in any other form. It creates a harmonious-seeming logic which an audience is less likely to question, and, therefore, more likely to agree with, at least subconsciously.

Evita said the name 'Perón' six times in a very short space. Whether intentional or not, this would have emphasised her key point: Perón is everything.

Eva then went on to use *kairos* when she invoked the significance of time before calling for everyone to make a vow. As you can imagine, her tricks worked and the audience went wild. People ritualistically chanted: 'Our lives for Perón!'

After this act of rhetorical mastery, Eva linked back to the idea of her life being left in shreds:

> Finally, compañeros, I thank you for all your prayers for my health; I thank you with all my heart. I hope that God hears the humble of my Fatherland so that I can quickly return to the struggle and be able to keep on fighting with Perón for you and with you for Perón until death. I don't ask or want anything for myself. My glory is and always will be to be Perón's shield and the flag of my people, and though I leave shreds of my life along the road, I know that you will pick up my name and will carry it to victory as a banner. I know that God is with us because he is with the humble and despises the arrogance of the oligarchy.

This is why victory will be ours. We will achieve it sooner or later, whatever the cost, whoever may fall.

My descamisados: I wanted to tell you many things but the doctors have forbidden me from speaking. I have you in my heart and tell you that it is certain my wish is that I will soon be back in the struggle, with more strength and love, to fight for this people which I love so much, as I love Perón. And I ask you just one thing: it's certain I will soon be with you, but if for health reasons I am not, take care of the general. Remain faithful to Perón as you've been until today, because this means being loyal to the Fatherland and loyal to yourselves. And to all the descamisados of the interior, I hold them closely, so very closely to my heart, and want them to know how much I love them.

Eva used a very powerful metaphor of herself as 'the flag of my people', which is then visualised as torn when, in the same sentence, she spoke of the 'shreds' of her life. The metaphor almost predicts her death and the impact it will have on the movement. She was very much aware that she was a symbol for the people of Argentina. She made herself that symbol, and then flaunted her status to shower her husband with glory and success.

By describing herself as a flag, Evita assumed the role of the pride of Argentina. This emotional crescendo led up to her request that, should she die, the people continue to follow Juan Perón. Even while facing death, she toed the party line and demonstrated love and support for her husband.

Because of her ill health, Eva Perón was speaking as if she were already a martyr. She was invoking very powerful *pathos* and using that to wield her influence towards her husband. We shouldn't waste too much time speculating as to whether she genuinely felt this way towards Juan or not, what we can confidently say is that her audience believed so.

Another interesting observation here is Eva's call for victory. She said: 'Victory will be ours. We will achieve it sooner or later, whatever the cost, whoever may fall'. This idea that victory costs lives is a common trope used to motivate people to want to die for their country, or to accept the deaths of others as a legitimate price for victory. Her words closely resemble Churchill's logic from his famous 1940 speech *Blood, Toil, Tears and Sweat*, when he said:

> You ask, what is our aim? I can answer in one word: It is victory, victory at all costs, victory in spite of all terror, victory, however long and hard the road may be; for without victory, there is no survival.

Speaking only 10 years later, Eva used such similar language. Why? Because these words, no matter the audience or the language, will motivate an audience to welcome struggle and pain into their lives as part of a greater purpose.

The Death of Eva Perón

In 1952, with her health rapidly deteriorating, Eva was appointed 'Spiritual Leader of the Nation' by the Argentine Congress. Shortly after receiving this honour, on 26 July 1952, she died of cancer.

The end of her life is wrapped in uncertainty. All signs suggest that it was unpleasant. Some say that she was given a lobotomy to ease her pain. Others go even further and speculate that her husband, unhappy with her influence, ordered the lobotomy.

Her husband, the man whom she adored and to whom she devoted all her efforts and aspirations in life, soon started a sexual relationship with a 14-year-old girl. He was eventually ousted from government in 1955 by his opponents and, while living in exile in Spain, was prosecuted for statutory rape. Eighteen years later, after the election of a Peronist President in 1973, Juan was allowed to return to Argentina. After the newly elected President resigned, another election was called, also in 1973, and Perón was once more elected as President. He ruled until his death in 1974.

After her death, Eva Perón's speeches and her life were studied in Argentine schools. Her autobiography, *La Razón de mi vida* (The Reason for My Life) – a true work of propaganda which was published shortly before her death – was mandatory reading for millions of school children.

Eva Perón's rhetoric shows us that the language of indoctrination isn't always about aggressively thumping a table while screaming into a microphone, or aggressively shaking a fist in the air. There is another side that is warm, comforting, and which is just as effective and dangerous as any other.

Jiang Qing (1914-991).
Photograph taken in 1976 by an unknown author.

13.
JIANG QING

One of the key features to successful speeches is to know your audience. Many speakers, especially the most tyrannical and manipulative, adapt their persona to match their audience's expectations.

To negotiate his position in a society of privilege and 'right to rule', the relatively low-born Napoleon branded himself as a divine emperor. Leaders in communist China, by contrast, defined themselves as children and 'screws' – a metaphor for something that is insignificant on its own but crucial for the construction of something greater. Don't be deceived by this self-deprecation: these leaders were just as deadly, powerful, and menacing as any others who projected themselves as mighty.

To demonstrate this, let's look at the narcissistic, manipulative, and deranged fourth wife of China's great revolutionary leader Chairman Mao Zedong, Jiang Qing.

About Jiang Qing

Jiang Qing was central to the Communist Party leadership, held office herself, and, through her affiliation with power, hunted down the people she loathed – and ended her career on trial for corruption, violence, and villainy. She was a great deal more than simply the wife of Mao, the 'Great Helmsman'. Prior to marrying Mao in 1938, Jiang Qing was a film actor with little involvement in politics. Soon after the wedding, she became Mao's secretary as he fought to take charge of China.

Revered as the closest thing that communism had to a deity, Mao was one of the founders of the Chinese Red Army, a formidable force that participated in the Chinese Civil War which cost the lives of millions of Chinese. The civil war stopped in 1937 when China was invaded by Japan – an even bloodier war which killed an estimated 20 million people. In 1945, with Japan's grip on China weakening and Japanese surrender imminent, the Chinese Civil War flared back into life. After Japan's surrender in 1945, Mao, alongside his newest wife, fought off the Chinese government and took full control of the Chinese mainland by 1949, leaving the defeated right-wing Kuomintang (KMT) party to retreat to the island of Taiwan.

By 1964, China had become a nuclear power, and Jiang Qing was its first lady. As such, everything she said, wore, and did was of national interest. Unlike the wives of many political leaders who stood in the background, smiled, and kept their composure, Jiang Qing was actively involved in politics and corruption, and gave speeches as both tool and master of the regime's propaganda. She was even the leader of a politically contentious radical Maoist group nicknamed the Gang of Four.

By the 1950s, Jiang Qing began wielding some real power as the head of the film section of the Communist Party's Propaganda Department.

In 1966, she rose to greater prominence when Mao launched what was called the Great Proletarian Cultural Revolution. In practice, this was an attempt to banish any cultural influences Mao disagreed with (for example, Western cinema), and force the masses to exclusively enjoy state-approved culture: culture which happened to align perfectly with Mao's own particular brand of communism. The deputy director of the Central Cultural Revolution Group was none other than his loyal wife, Jiang Qing. She was merciless in her implementation of this sweeping cultural upheaval, which sparked mass civil unrest and violence. Many intellectuals and elderly people who spoke out against the reforms were beaten to death by zealous troops operating under Jiang's orders. With her newly appointed official role in the Chinese government and the ear of Mao, Jiang Qing was politically untouchable and protected from any criticism or challenge to her authority.

Records suggest that Jiang was rotten from the very start. One of her hobbies was to watch Hollywood movies in private screenings. Yet she banned anyone else in China from watching the same movies because they were 'bourgeoisie'. Some may feel that this is an indication of mild hypocrisy rather than full-blown villainy: she was guilty of both. Once comfortably in power, Jiang wreaked havoc on people she didn't like. She had the children of her political opponents tortured and murdered; she went out of her way to destroy the lives of people who had upset her decades earlier during her acting career; and she whimsically used her position of influence to ruin and end tens of thousands of people's lives. Despite her wickedness, or perhaps because of it, she continued to rise and, in 1969, gained a seat on China's highest policy-making body, the Politburo.

Her Speeches

Most speeches will open with the speaker attempting to assert their *ethos*. By establishing character and credibility, a speaker can usually expect an audience to be more attentive. In the opening of a speech on 14 September 1968, at the official 'Reception for the Representatives of the Beijing Workers Propaganda Team and the People's Liberation Army Propaganda Team,' Jiang did just this. She said:

> My dear comrades! Salute to you, comrades! [I want to] learn from you, comrades!

> I am an ordinary Communist, a little pupil of Chairman Mao, and a little pupil of the broad masses. I have to learn from my dear comrades.

In the opening sentence, Jiang began by praising her audience with a classic use of *comprobatio* with a *tricolon of epistrophe* (repeating the end of a sentence or clause three times in a way which complimented the audience). By explicitly stating that she wanted to learn from her audience, she was attempting to win their favour and imply that they were somehow superior to her. Knowing what we do of Jiang, we can assume that she did not actually believe this.

After praising and saluting her audience, Jiang immediately established her character with a *tricolon* of statements around her *ethos*. She claimed to be:

1. An ordinary Communist

2. A little pupil of Chairman Mao
3. A little pupil of the broad masses

This *tricolon of ethos* is significant because it was also a use of *logos*. Jiang Qing presented her audience with a loose syllogism which implicitly – perhaps subliminally – signalled to her audience that a good communist, the kind who serves the masses, was also the kind that learnt from Mao. If you reverse the logical implication, she said: 'If you do not follow Mao you are not a true Communist'. She was echoing the regime's attempts to force Mao's style of communism onto the masses.

As well as presenting the audience with a little logic, this *tricolon of ethos* also established Jiang's own credibility. Unlike other leaders before her who flaunted their high status, Jiang had to do the opposite; she had to present herself as being unprivileged and proletariat, because that is what her audience wanted to hear. To do this, she suggested her *ethos* was that of an insignificant pupil.

A few sentences into the speech she reinforced her own insignificance when she metaphorically stated: 'I am only a small screw!' This metaphor suggests, in true communist fashion, that she simply performed a useful but unglamorous role in securing the integrity of the state. This presented her as a party member who was equally modest as anyone else in the audience.

Aside from using *ethos* to define her own character, Jiang used it to vilify her opponent through *argumentum ad hominem*. When deploying *argumentum ad hominem* there are usually two common routes: you vilify a named individual; or you vilify a mysterious generic outsider who represents the enemy. Generally speaking, vilifying the mysterious 'other' works well in the absence of a universally agreed villainous individual.

Throughout history, power-hoarders have created a mysterious enemy 'bogeyman' to scare the masses into submission. In the context of revolutionary China, Jiang made her bogeyman the right-wing capitalist.

In a speech from 1967, Jiang said:

> How do things stand at present in this connection? First, there are the Party capitalists in authority, in addition to the landlords, rich peasants, counter-revolutionaries, wicked people and Rightists, in addition to US spies, Soviet spies, Japanese spies, and Kuomintang spies — all of them are bent on destroying us. With so many black hands hidden behind their backs, it is not easy for you to discern them. Appearing either as ultra-'Leftists' or as Rightists, they are set to undermine the Party Central Committee headed by Chairman Mao. This shall never be permitted and those who do so are doomed to failure.

The first thing to note here is her use of *abundantia*. She variously listed her enemies as 'Party capitalists in authority, in addition to the landlords, rich peasants, counter-revolutionaries, wicked people and Rightists, in addition to US spies, Soviet spies, Japanese spies, and Kuomintang spies'. The reason for using *abundantia* in this instance was two-fold: first, it emphasised how many enemies were ranged against Communist China; second, it allowed the audience to share their hatred of any of the groups that they were personally aggrieved by. If one had a particular hatred towards rich landlords (to pick a random example), this speech might have triggered one's anger.

After listing the various enemies of the people, Jiang then deployed a common trope of hate, by saying that they were hidden among them. This trope of a hidden enemy has been deployed throughout history, from the Romans to the Nazis. Perhaps due to instinct, or perhaps due to social conditioning, people have always feared that which they cannot see. You may remember that Eva Perón did something similar when she stated that 'the enemies work in the shade of treason and sometimes are hidden behind a smile or an extended hand'.

Jiang Qing's message to her audience was: *you are under threat, the enemy is strong, you must be vigilant.* As you might imagine, it worked exactly as she planned. People in China were constantly on the lookout for the hidden enemy. This led to a puritanical purge in society of anyone deemed to have any political views other than those sanctioned by the establishment. Many innocent people were maliciously accused of being bourgeoisie by their neighbours and colleagues, and were punished severely, with punishments ranging from having their hair forcibly cut off to being beaten to death.

The Legend of the Red Lantern

Rhetoric is more than just speeches, edicts and pamphlets, and can be found throughout culture. The corner of culture that Jiang Qing knew best was the theatre. Her acting past, combined with her position on the Politburo, allowed her to reinvent Chinese theatre in a way that benefited the regime and brainwashed the masses.

As China's cultural revolution expunged all traces of what was seen as bourgeois, new forms of culture arose. One of them, masterminded by Jiang, was communist revolutionary opera. These ballet-infused operas told narratives of a humble protagonist (usually a woman) who overcame turmoil to promote communist ideology.

While traditional opera would tell the tale of some emperor or high-ranking aristocrat, communist operas focused on the struggles of ordinary people and the glory of the revolutionary forces. They glorified violence, martyrdom, and served one purpose: to educate, indoctrinate, and manipulate the masses of China into submission. Think *Swan Lake* meets *West Side Story*, but with the good guys dressed as communist soldiers and the villains usually wearing Japanese uniforms.

There were a total of eight state-approved operas in China. They were incredibly popular; perhaps because they were one of the few permitted forms of entertainment. Records tell of children singing their favourite revolutionary opera songs in the streets as they walked to school. Songs included lines such as: 'I won't quit until all the beasts are killed!'

We shall look at one state-approved opera overseen by Jiang, *The Legend of the Red Lantern*. *The Legend of the Red Lantern* is set in Japanese-occupied China and follows a band of communist underground rebels who are betrayed to the Japanese by a traitor. The communists have to endure torture at the hands of the Japanese to keep secret a code which is crucial to the success of the communists. The Japanese authorities are denigrated, while the Chinese revolutionary forces are glorified. This contrast is emphasised through the narrative and language, and through the music and costume, with grotesque features for the villains and heroic music for the protagonists.

Towards the beginning of the script, a stage direction sums up the ethos of the opera. The character Granny is meant to represent the older generation: respectable, caring, and wise. The stage direction reads:

[Granny looks at the scarf. Revolutionary memories float before her eyes: hatred, old and new, for the enemy comes to her mind.]

As well as the explicit attempt to evoke emotion through *pathos*, these short stage directions use *antithesis* (contrast), *kairos* (the invoking of time), and *argumentum ad hominem* (an attack against someone's character).

Ultimately, Jiang Qing wanted her Maoist followers to feel the same sentiments as the character of the grandmother in the opera, and the entire play was designed to invoke hatred of the Japanese, as well as towards Chinese traitors to the communist cause.

The rhetoric of the stage directions, as symbolic and interesting as they may be, are nothing compared to the speeches made by the characters. A good example of *argumentum ad hominem* in song is in the grandmother's speech to her granddaughter outlining what the Japanese had done to her real parents (the girl, Tiemei, has just discovered that she was adopted). The Granny says:

Be brave and listen.

In the strike those devils murdered your father and mother,

Li Yu-ho worked untiringly for the revolution;

he swore to follow in the martyrs' steps, to keep

the red lantern burning;

he staunched his words, buried the dead and went on with the fight.

Now the Japanese brigands are burning, killing and looting, before our eyes your dad was taken away to prison;

remember this debt of blood and tears,

> be brave and determined to settle accounts with the enemy,
>
> a debt of blood must be paid with blood.

Here, the character Granny uses a range of triadic repetition to emphasise her messages. The first *tricolon* arrives when Granny characterises the *ethos* of the father by saying, 'he staunched his words, buried the dead and went on with the fight'. The second use of *tricolon* is when Granny uses *argumentum ad hominem* and *anadiplosis* (repeating a word at the end of a clause and at the beginning of the next) to vilify the Japanese 'brigands' who she says are 'burning, killing and looting'. Jiang Qing (or whoever wrote the operas under her instruction) no doubt chose these three verbs from the semantic field of war and destruction to reinforce the hatred of the enemy: the same sentiment of hate which Jiang used in her speeches.

It is worth noting that Granny, the moderate voice of aged wisdom, ends this song to her adopted granddaughter with a violent call to action: 'a debt of blood must be paid with blood.'

The lantern in *The Legend of the Red Lantern* was a metaphor for the revolutionary spirit that was passed down the generations. While the protagonists of these revolutionary operas were usually young women, the antagonists were predominantly male. In *The Legend of the Red Lantern*, the protagonist, a 17-year-old girl named Teimei, sings a number of passionate songs glorifying the communists and acknowledging her own duty to promote communism and battle against the enemies. In response to Granny's speech above, Teimei sings:

> My father is as steadfast as the pine,
>
> a communist who fears nothing under the sun.
>
> Following in your footsteps I shall never waver.

> The red lantern we hold high, and it shines
>
> on my father fighting those wild beasts.
>
> Generation after generation we shall fight on,
>
> never leaving the field until all the wolves are killed.
>
> [Tiemei and Granny hold high the red lantern in a dramatic pose.
>
> It casts a radiant red light.]

The willingness to die for the communist revolution is explicitly glorified towards the end of the opera when Granny and Li (the adopted father) are executed by the Japanese sergeant (the rather obvious antagonist). The stage directions read as follows:

> Sergeant: shoot them!
>
> [to the militant strains of 'the Internationale' the three revolutionaries of three generations, head high, walk up the slope, defying death. They go out].
>
> [Japanese gendarmes follow.]
>
> [Silence. Offstage, Li shouts: 'Down with Japanese imperialism!' 'Long live the Chinese Communist Party!' The three of them shout with their arm raised 'Long live Chairman Mao!']
>
> [A volley of shots. Two Japanese Gendarmes drag Tiemei in and throw her down].

The Japanese officials murder her father and grandmother in front of her in an attempt to get the code. But (spoiler!) Tiemei manages to get the code to the communist rebels.

At the end of the opera, Tiemei sings an emotional and powerful promise for revenge. She sings about her rage and how she will never surrender and is willing to die for the cause. The entire song – which echoes Tiemei's character development – is clearly composed to elicit pride, anger, and a lust for revolutionary vengeance; in one word: *pathos*.

Even this brief introduction to the soliloquies, the dialogues, and the stage directions from *The Legend of the Red Lantern* shows us that this is more than mindless entertainment. This is a crafted political tool which sought to indoctrinate the communist classes through the guise of entertainment. Impressively, it got away with a much more exaggerated application of rhetorical schemes and tropes than a speech could have done.

All eight of the revolutionary operas engineered by Jiang Qing were emotionally charged propaganda pieces intended to imbue the audience, young and old, with the feeling of revolutionary empowerment.

The End of Jiang Qing

Mao Zedong died in September 1976 and left in his wake the sort of power vacuum that commonly follows dangerous political instability. Jiang, one of the most powerful officials in the Chinese Communist Party, tried to cling on to power; however, in doing so, she made a number of enemies who eventually got the upper hand and had her arrested. She was charged with being responsible for the civil unrest during the Cultural Revolution and put on trial: a show trial. Her prosecution claimed that she had persecuted 727,420 Chinese citizens and was personally responsible for 34,274 Chinese deaths. While under arrest, reports suggest that she was tortured, beaten, and starved.

In true Jiang fashion, she behaved dramatically throughout the trial – which was televised – making grand statements and singing patriotic songs. On one occasion, she gave such a dramatic speech that the authorities decided not to broadcast the show that day. Little is known about what she said. Some reports say she challenged the people in the room by vaunting her status and achievements. Reportedly, she recalled being the only female comrade on the front lines with Mao when the Kuomintang (The KMT political party) advanced on the city of Yan'an (a city in the Shaanxi province located in central China) in 1947. After reminding the courtroom about this fact, she retorted with 'Where were you then?' And then stated: 'You are trying Chairman Mao's Wife'. In her final public moment, she used her rhetorical arsenal to try and defend herself by invoking her *ethos* with a rhetorical question (*erotema*).

Unfortunately for Jiang, her attempts to exonerate herself failed and she was sentenced to death with a two-year reprieve; a sentence that was later changed to life imprisonment. In 1991, she was transferred from prison to a hospital, where she took her own life.

Jiang Qing is a prime example of how the power of rhetoric can indoctrinate the masses. More importantly, it shows us leaders can co-opt culture to enforce an ideology.

Mobutu Sese Seko (1930-1997).
Photograph taken in 1983 by Frank Hall as President
Mobutu met US Secretary of Defense Caspar Weinberger
in the Pentagon.

14.
MOBUTU

Violence and exploitation had wracked the Congo long before it was ruled over by Joseph-Désiré Mobutu.

In 1885, a tyrannical European monarch called Leopold II of Belgium – cousin to Queen Victoria – brutally seized the Congolese landmass in the heart of Africa and declared it to be his private property. He named it Congo Free State. Despite the use of the word 'Free', there was very little freedom in the Congo. Unlike other European colonies which were ruled by another country, this 'nation' was privately owned by Leopold II, who ruled as an absolute monarch. Mostly through punishment and malnutrition, around half of the Congolese population are estimated to have perished under Leopold II's rule.

In 1908, the year before Leopold II's death, the ownership of the country was transferred from the Belgian king to the country of Belgium and renamed Belgian Congo.

After more turbulence, death, and suffering as a colony of Belgium, Belgian Congo finally gained its independence in 1960.

After a significant series of messy politics, on 24 June 1960, a 35-year-old man named Patrice Lumumba was declared the first Congolese Prime Minister. Lumumba, a strong campaigner for independence, was known as an eloquent orator who gave powerful speeches.

He was so good at speaking that some of his speeches were given off the cuff without any preparation. During the Independence Day ceremony, the then King of Belgium, King Baudouin, praised the 'genius' of Leopold II, his great uncle. Perhaps in a state of outrage, Lumumba – who was not scheduled to speak – stood up and said:

> For this independence of the Congo, although being proclaimed today by agreement with Belgium, an amicable country, with which we are on equal terms, no Congolese worthy of the name will ever be able to forget that it was by fighting that it has been won, a day-to-day fight, an ardent and idealistic fight, a fight in which we were spared neither privation nor suffering, and for which we gave our strength and our blood.
>
> We are proud of this struggle, of tears, of fire, and of blood, to the depths of our being, for it was a noble and just struggle, and indispensable to put an end to the humiliating slavery which was imposed upon us by force.

You can imagine that King Baudouin of Belgium and his delegation disliked this improvisation, which is packed with rhetorical techniques.

Shortly after Lumumba's appointment, violence broke out in the fragile newly-founded nation. It is often attributed to four words written on a blackboard: 'before independence = after independence'. They were written by Émile Janssen, a white Belgian commander, who told his Congolese troops that nothing changed and that Belgians were still in control. The Congolese troops started a riot. The following day, Lumumba sacked Janssen and gave all Congolese soldiers a pay increase, but the rioting had already spread to the Lower Congo. As white officers and their families were taken captive, Europeans began to flee the country. There was public anger, political instability, and a power vacuum: the perfect breeding ground for a dictator's rise to power.

Lumumba's personal aide was a man named Joseph-Désiré Mobutu. Mobutu helped negotiate the release of the white commanders and their families. Shortly after that he was promoted to Colonel, and shortly after that to Army Chief of Staff.

As time progressed more violence and chaos broke out in what became known as the Congo Crisis (1960-1965). In an attempt to restore order, Lumumba turned to the world's superpowers. After not receiving any substantial help from the United States of America, he turned to the Soviet Union, despite not being inclined towards communism. The Western world did not react well to this and began to put pressure on powerful individuals within the newly founded Congolese state to overthrow Lumumba.

Seeing his chance, Mobutu, the Army Chief of Staff, staged a coup and declared himself leader. Lumumba was trapped inside his residence, where the only thing keeping him safe from Mobutu's soldiers was a UN peacekeeping force.

Having lost nearly all of his power, Lumumba – who still insisted that he was in charge – wanted to start giving speeches to rally his support. But he couldn't do so from his residence. In late November 1960, Lumumba escaped and fled towards the north of the country, where he had more support.

On the journey, he stopped off a few times and managed to give some of his famous speeches. But Mobutu's soldiers captured him before he made it to safety. In his possession, Lumumba had a copy of a speech he was planning to deliver. In it, he claimed that he was still the rightful Congolese leader.

After beating him up and mockingly reciting elements of the speech to him, Mobutu's men scrunched the speech into a paper ball and forced it into Lumumba's mouth. By forcing Lumumba to eat his speech, Mobutu and his men not only showed their own physical dominance, but mockingly acknowledged Lumumba's undoubted rhetorical advantage.

After this public display of humiliation, which was recorded on video and broadcast across the globe, Lumumba disappeared. He had been killed by a firing squad in January 1961 and buried. To prevent him from having a burial site, his corpse was dug up days later, cut into small pieces, and dissolved in sulphuric acid.

Mobutu did not assume leadership of the country during this time but instead supported the creation of a new government. With backing from the United States of America, Mobutu spent four years quashing all the various rebellions across the country and brought the Congo Crisis to an end in 1965. The Congolese government appointed him Major General.

Despite not being the political leader, Mobutu was now the most powerful man in the Congo. Six days after being appointed Major General, in 1965, he staged a second military coup and dismissed the President and Prime Minister and assumed power himself. One of the first things he did was publicly execute political opponents in front of a live crowd of tens of thousands.

Mobutu reigned for 32 years. During his rule, he banned Western clothing and he weaponised terror to control his citizens. He institutionalised rape and torture and he embezzled billions of dollars from his own country's finances. He was once described as being the last political dinosaur of Africa.

The Ethos of Papa Mobutu

How did a man like Mobutu manage to maintain power for so long? Some might jump to the conclusion that he was ruthless and maintained his power through force. Things are rarely this simple, though. In his book *The Dialects of Oppression in Zaire*, the political scientist Michael Schatzberg says: 'No state can long exist on mere coercion; leaders must persuade people to accept, willingly or with resignation, the reigning political order'. Mobutu may have used force and coercion to rise to the top, but there was something more that kept him in power for 32 years.

The way that Mobutu did this was partly – one could argue significantly – through his use of rhetoric. Mobutu's secret weapon was *ethos*: the rhetorical feature that allows a speaker to define their character to their audience. What was Mobutu's persona of choice? It was Papa Mobutu: the father, the chief, the god.

Any dedicated dictator has to have an appropriate name and Joseph-Désiré Mobutu decided he needed a rebrand. He declared that European names were bad and instead promoted African identity. He ordered people to change European names and, in 1972, changed his own name to Mobutu Sese Seko Kuku Ngbendu wa za Banga – a name which loosely translates as 'the warrior who knows no defeat because of his endurance and inflexible will and is all-powerful, leaving fire in his wake as he goes from conquest to conquest'.

His new name evoked the narrative of supernatural powers, a right to rule, and a habit for victory. He also renamed the entire country from the Democratic Republic of the Congo to the Republic of Zaire. 'Congo' is the European interpretation of the name of the mighty river which runs through the country. 'Zaire' was an older name that was used for the same river. Ironically, the name 'Zaire' has Portuguese etymological roots, so was not as African as Mobutu pretended. Nevertheless, it was a symbolic move away from the Belgian influence that had terrorised the people for so long.

Very few people on this planet have the authority and power to rename a nation: an act that signals control, or perhaps even ownership. One could argue that, by renaming the entire nation, Mobutu was signalling to everyone in his country that it was under his complete control. His people were no longer Congolese, they were now Zairian.

Mobutu's use of imagery and ethos didn't end with his name. Throughout his reign, he constantly pushed different images and metaphors to portray himself as brilliant and everyone he didn't like as worthless animals.

On one occasion Mobutu said: 'The chief is the chief. He is the eagle who flies high and cannot be touched by the spit of the toad'. These 22 words alone tell us a lot about Mobutu's *ethos*. But they also show us some of his rhetorical flamboyance. In this short extract, Mobutu contrasts the eagle and the toad in the form of a *zoomorphic antithesis*. Vivid imagery of this sort is known as *energia*. It is the same feature that Attila the Hun used when describing broken bodies in the battle field, but in a very different way. Criticising your enemies by branding them as spitting toads – or, indeed, any other unpleasant thing – is a form of *argumentum ad hominem*. The metaphor is clear and powerful: Mobutu is good and those who oppose him are bad.

The *ethos* of chief was a mantle that Mobutu wore throughout his reign alongside that of shepherd and father (father, perhaps, being the most significant). In 1983, Mobutu proclaimed a general amnesty for all political prisoners. He declared:

> We live on the earth of men and the large family of the MPR[1] today numbers close to 30 million souls. In every family, bad boys – difficult children – are not absent…
>
> My constant worry has always been to give each son, each daughter of this country, the opportunity to bring his small contribution to the work of national recovery. The chief that I am is not only for the good citizens, but also, and perhaps even more, for those who are less so.
>
> And if a chief must know how to punish, I believe that a pardon is sometimes necessary. There is not only the prodigal child who deserts the parental roof whose return one day is possibly awaited, there is also the lost sheep who leaves the herd that the master is going to find…

In this one extract, Mobutu is the father, the shepherd and the chief: all of which are positions of control, authority and power.

It wasn't just through his own words that Mobutu propagated his ethos. The image of Mobutu as father and chief of the nation was institutionalised in media, education, and all aspects of Zarian life.

---

[1] MPR (Mouvement Populaire de la Révolution in French or Popular Movement of the Revolution in English) was Mobutu's political party. Every citizen of Zaire was a member. Every member had a responsibility to the nation and the father. It was no coincidence that Mobutu used the metaphor of the MPR as a family. He wanted 30 million people to consider him as their patriarch.

In elementary school, schoolchildren would have to spend the first 15 minutes of everyday dancing and chanting 'One party, one country, one father, Mobutu, Mobutu'. This is obviously a *tricolon*, but the repetition of 'one' at the beginning also makes it *anaphora*: both of which are powerful forms of repetition to reinforce a message. Less common is the use of *epizeuxis*, the immediate repetition of a single word for emphasis (in this case 'Mobutu, Mobutu').

To further emphasise his position, the daily state-controlled news broadcasts would always begin with a clip of Mobutu descending from the clouds. Mobutu was not just a father: he was a god.

Mobutu's mother was called Mama Yemo and was often referred to in the press as mother of all Zairians. It is not unusual for dictators to glorify their relatives to emphasise their status as being above others. Julius Caesar did so at his aunt Julia's funeral when he said: 'The family of my aunt Julia is descended by her mother from the kings and on her father's side is akin to the immortal gods'. This is a use of what is often called genetic fallacy: making a claim that something is true because of its origins.

Mobutu often liked to attack his opposition, and loved laying into the European colonists who had exploited his country. This sort of *argumentum ad hominem* was a staple in the rhetoric of Papa Mobutu, who built collective hatred towards his enemies in order to justify his own levels of power.

We've already looked at Mobutu using *zoomorphic ad hominem* when he called his opponents spitting toads. He also deployed this tactic in one of his UN speeches when he said:

> In 1885 the great slave-traders of the period met in Berlin and, like vultures, carved up the African continent among themselves [...] The exploitation of the blacks would not be sporadic;

> it would now become systematic, permanent and definitive by the pure and simple appropriation of the African territories by the slave-traders.

The failings of powerful nations are often used to justify atrocities by weaker ones. Mobutu would often argue that what he was doing was relatively harmless compared to what the Western world had done in the not-too-distant past. For this reason, it was always in his interests to reference the slavery, corruption, and Western exploitation of African territories. *Argumentum ad hominem*, in this context, could silence potential criticism of Zaire as it risked making its opponents look like hypocrites. The reason that this false logic works is that much of the world seeks to position any conflict parties into the oppressor and the oppressed. This is a false dichotomy which presents two fixed places ignoring the possibility of a nation being both the oppressor and the oppressed. If Mobutu could make the larger enemies seem like the oppressors, in many people's minds that would excuse the wrongdoings of Zaire, which takes on victim status.

In the same speech, Mobutu used *abundantia* to emphasise his messages. We can see this when he said:

> Our ancestors were not considered as men, or even as beings with intelligence and feeling. They were considered as a set of muscles fit for mechanical labour such as we expect from an animal – a horse, a buffalo, a donkey or an ox.

In the same speech, he also said:

> 1960 to 1965 were dreadful years for us and we are forced to recognize that anarchy, chaos, disorder, blindness and incapacity prevailed in Zaire.

The use of 'anarchy, chaos, disorder, blindness and incapacity' is another use of *abundantia*. This repetition allowed Mobutu to emphasise his *argumentum ad hominem* criticism of the Western nations – a good example of how one rhetorical feature can be used to bolster another.

Mobutu's metaphors – which were so integral to his rhetorical campaigns – were further enhanced by strategic uses of various forms of repetition.

The final point I will touch on in this chapter, is that Mobutu, like so many others, would look to the great examples throughout history to find inspiration for his words.

Mobutu once said:

> My country is ready to undertake this sacred struggle, whatever may be the sacrifices involved. And we shall never retreat, regardless of what may happen, regardless of what it may cost.

It is hard not to spot the similarities to Churchill's 1940 *We shall fight on the beaches* speech when the British prime minister said:

> ...we shall defend our Island, whatever the cost may be, we shall fight on the beaches, we shall fight on the landing grounds, we shall fight in the fields and in the streets, we shall fight in the hills; we shall never surrender.

Similarly to Eva Perón's Labour Day speech in which she repeated 'victory', it is highly likely that this part of Mobutu's speech was inspired by Churchill's famous war speech. Tyrants will often echo the wording of a famous speech that many people under their rule are likely to have heard.

The End of Mobutu

As with most tyrants and dictators, maintaining power when you get older can be challenging, especially if your regime is brutal and needs constant enforcement through violence. As with so many dictators before him, Mobutu lost his grip on the people. The turning point was when he meddled in the Rwandan Genocide, which began in 1994. Mobutu sided with the Hutu aggressors who had slaughtered 800,000 Tutsis. He started off by allowing the Hutus space in Zaire, and then, in 1996, banished all Tutsi from his nation. These actions caused unrest and resistance that helped to trigger a civil war, which became known as the First Congo War. Mobutu, now riddled with cancer, lost the war. On 23 May 1997, Mobutu was officially exiled to Rabat, Morocco. On the same day, Zaire was renamed the Democratic Republic of the Congo. Mobutu was gone, his *ethos* was destroyed, and the first steps were taken to dismantle his legacy.

Mobutu went into exile with both his wife Bobi Ladawa and her twin sister (his mistress) Kosia Ngama. He died of cancer in exile on 7 September 1997.

Whether his people believed his claims of grandeur and divinity is hard to know, but what we can say is that those who saw through his words were too afraid to speak up. No one wanted to call out their father in front of their 30 million siblings, especially when they knew his cruelty.

*Indira Gandhi (1917-1984).
Official portrait taken in 1983.*

15.
INDIRA GANDHI

Indira Gandhi is not in this book just because of her electoral malpractice. Gandhi is considered to be a dictator because of her response to a High Court ruling which convicted her of that malpractice and subsequently banned her from politics.

Gandhi was an elected member of the Indian Parliament in 1964, and Prime Minister in 1966. On 12 June 1975, a High Court passed judgement that she had committed electoral malpractice and could therefore no longer have a constituency seat in parliament. As she was no longer a member of the Indian parliament, she lost her right to vote. Despite this, she was allowed to continue as Prime Minister. Naturally, people were unhappy that a politician convicted of corruption had remained in power and mass protests erupted across India.

How can a leader of a democratic nation respond to such a conviction? There are two options: the first is they accept the verdict and step down peacefully; the second is that they cause chaos and secure power through whatever means necessary. Gandhi chose the latter. She wasn't going to be stopped by the judicial system or democracy. So, she broke them.

How can a prime minister of a democratic country destroy democracy? They do it in the name of whatever the people hold dear. In this case: democracy itself. In the name of Indian democracy, Gandhi gave herself emergency powers and the right to rule by decree. Thus she overruled democracy and became India's first dictator.

With her new power, Gandhi overruled the Indian High and Supreme Courts and arrested her political rivals. She even cut off electricity to the offices of newspapers who dared to criticise her. As a newly founded dictator, Gandhi announced the dawn of the new age of tyranny in a dramatic speech broadcast to all of India.

On 26 June 1975, Gandhi gave a speech on the radio, where she said:

> I am sure you are all conscious of the deep and widespread conspiracy which has been brewing ever since I began introducing certain progressive measures of benefit to the common man and woman of India. In the name of democracy, it has sought to negate the very functioning of democracy. Duly elected governments have not been allowed to function, and in some cases, force has been used to compel members to resign in order to dissolve lawfully elected assemblies.

Ironically, she accused her enemies of doing the very same thing she had just done: using force to dissolve lawfully elected assemblies. But in a masterful stroke of rhetoric, Gandhi, while silently assassinating democracy, presented herself as its defender. This form of *argumentum ad hominem* was used to strengthen her own *ethos*. By branding her opponents as the enemies of democracy, she reinforced her own image as its defender.

She also asserted that her policies were benefiting common men and women. She said this because, in a time of revolt and political upheaval, the most powerful ally a leader can have is common men and women. That sentiment was further reinforced through her use of direct address.

Later in the speech, she went on to defend her name and claim that these new powers were not for her own benefit but for democracy's. She said:

> All manner of false allegations have been hurled at me. The Indian people have known me since my childhood. All my life has been in the service of our people. This is not a personal matter. It is not important whether I remain Prime Minister or not. However, the institution of the Prime Minister is important, and the political attempt to denigrate it is not in the interest of democracy or of the nation.

Gandhi united the rhetorical forces of *logos, ethos, and pathos* in one stroke of manipulation. Her insistence that the institution of Prime Minister was weakened by legal checks and balances is a distorted logical argument suggesting that democracy is compromised when the elected leader can't do what they want. This was her use of *logos* (invoking logic to make your argument).

Her *ethos* (crafting of character) – which she already began building – was further defined as defender of the people when she invoked her childhood. She was the daughter of Jawaharlal Nehru, the first Prime Minister of the newly founded Indian state. She was, therefore, involved in public life from a young age. This recalling of her childhood relationship with the people of India was intended to build their trust and, perhaps, elicit some form of nostalgia. This is where we find the third of the main branches of rhetoric: *pathos* (an appeal to emotion).

A few sentences later, Gandhi hit her audience with a series of rhetorical questions in an attempt to prove her case that drastic action was needed to preserve democracy. She said:

> How can any government worth the name stand by and allow the country's stability to be imperilled? The actions of a few are endangering the rights of the vast majority. Any situation which weakens the capacity of the national government to act decisively inside the country is bound to encourage dangers from outside. It is our paramount duty to safeguard unity and stability. The nation's integrity demands firm action.

There are two uses of *antithesis* in this section. The first is when she mentions that 'the actions of a few are endangering the rights of the vast majority'. This *antithesis* would have been designed to anger the people of India: after all, it was their rights that were being endangered, or so she claimed. The second use of *antithesis* was when she spoke of how weak internal policy could encourage dangers from outside ('Any situation which weakens the capacity of the national government to act decisively inside the country is bound to encourage dangers from outside'). Her audience would have been very much aware of the threats from outside, as during her time there were worrying conflicts with both China and Pakistan.

By stating that the nation had no integrity or wasn't 'worth the name' if it didn't have a powerful leader, she was encouraging her audience to make her one. Patriotism is a powerful form of *pathos*, and the promise of glory (which is essentially what she was promising), is a good way to empower an audience to accept dangerous shifts in power.

No matter where you go in the world, people's pride in their country often makes them vulnerable to the temptations of extremism. Dictators, people who are well aware of these vulnerabilities, often use that emotive pride to justify cuts to democracy, just as Gandhi did here. *Pathos* is, as you now know, the most powerful rhetorical tool for any speaker, tyrannical or otherwise. It is because of this power that Gandhi used it so much in her speech. She knew that if she managed to overpower her audience's reason with emotion, she would get away with her high-stakes power grab.

Analysing this rhetorically, it is clear to see what she was doing. But, at the time, amid all the political chaos, it would have been very different for people who were listening to that speech live. People would have had conflicting emotions, conflicting reports, and conflicting priorities.

The Time of Emergency Power

During the 21 months she held emergency powers, Gandhi committed a number of atrocities. One of these was the mass sterilisation in 1976 of 6.2 million men and teenage boys in India – mostly men and boys from impoverished backgrounds. Gandhi had been pressured by the World Bank and the International Monetary Fund to take action to stop India's population from growing uncontrollably. She asked her son, Sanjay Gandhi, to lead the forced sterilisation. It was rough, brutal, and often took place in unhygienic camps on dingy tables. Teenage boys and elderly men in their late 70s alike were forced to go through the procedures, in most cases against their will.

There were reports from the time of men being forced to undergo the sterilisation process twice because authorities didn't believe that they had done it. Citizens were beaten, coerced, and bullied by authorities into being sterilised. There are accounts of civil servants having their pay withheld until they were sterilised. It is estimated that thousands of people died as a result of botched vasectomies conducted in unhygienic practices.

Twenty-one months later, feeling confident that she had successfully suppressed any real opposition, Gandhi let go of her emergency powers and held an election – one that she dramatically and unexpectedly lost. She was unseated as Prime Minister. Despite no longer being Prime Minister, she was once more an MP – the earlier ban was lifted – and she was now leader of the opposition. The new Janata coalition government put Gandhi on trial for corruption and eventually had her arrested. Her arrest meant she was automatically stripped of her seat in parliament. Despite thinking this would be popular, the move backfired against the Janata coalition.

Gandhi's support only grew because of her arrest and pro-Gandhi activists caused political instability in the Janata coalition. Gandhi was released and the newly formed coalition crumbled. An election was called and Gandhi was re-elected. In January 1980, she once again became Prime Minister.

Operation Blue Star and the Independence Day Speech

During her second term, several different groups and regions campaigned to secede from India. One such movement was the Sikh separatist movement which climaxed in June 1984. Sikhs were (and still are) a minority in India, a predominantly Hindu nation. Armed Sikh militants fortified themselves inside the Harmandir Sahib (also known as the Golden Temple), which is the holiest site for Sikhs and visited by many pilgrims.

Gandhi decided to remove the separatist militants using heavy-handed force. Deploying tanks, helicopters, and heavy artillery, the Indian army laid siege to the fortified temple. As there was no warning that a curfew and siege was going to take place, and the communications for the region were shut down, the temple and surrounding area was filled with innocent pilgrims and worshippers. During the siege of the Golden Temple, up to 10,000 Sikh civilians are estimated to have died along with the Sikh militants. The Golden Temple was left in ruins.

How do you calm a people when the country is recovering from a government-ordered massacre? You present them with a message they can all support. In this case, it was independence from Britain, the former colonial ruler.

Two months after the devastation of Operation Bluestar came India's Independence Day, a day which is traditionally marked with a speech. Independence is a strong and emotive subject: one which corrupt leaders often invoke when they want to manipulate the masses into doing what they want. In a particularly rhetorical flourish, Gandhi said in her Independence Day speech, in New Delhi, on 15 August 1984:

> If we have achieved independence, we should not rest peacefully that we have now achieved independence. We have to struggle always to maintain it. We have to protect this flame of independence from every storm, from every gust of wind, we have to save it with our hard work.

Following the political turmoil of recent months, Gandhi was attempting to motivate the people of India out of disgruntlement and into action. Often, the more desperate someone is to achieve something, the more rhetoric they flourish. And this relatively short extract was packed.

The first thing worth noting is the *anaphoric* repetition of 'we' at the start of three consecutive clauses. Such inclusive language sends the message that India is united – an important message to deliver given the recent internal divisions with the Sikh communities.

The three-part repetition of 'We have to...' at the opening of consecutive clauses is a *tricolon of anaphora* (repetition at the start of a clause, sentence or paragraph). The verbs used in this *tricolon* were 'struggle', 'protect', and 'save', all words associated with independence. Using multiple words which (in this context) mean similar things is a use of *abundantia*. Gandhi also used the repetition of 'independence' at the end of two consecutive clauses, an example of *epistrophe*.

Gandhi's message itself is boring and weak. Ultimately, it can be distilled to: *you need to work hard*. It is her rhetorical repetitions that made this message powerful. But was this speech enough to begin the process of healing the rifts with the Sikh community?

Securing a Dynasty

Gandhi seemed to be making efforts not to be too openly anti-Sikh. When her security advisors told her that it was unwise to have Sikh men as part of her security team, she reportedly dismissed the idea of removing them, thinking that it would be antagonistic.

It was, however, clear that some people wanted her dead: not just people from the Indian Sikh population but groups all over India and beyond. Gandhi was beginning to realise that her assassination was a very real possibility. An important part of being a true tyrant is laying the foundations for a dynasty. Years before the Golden Temple massacre, Gandhi pulled the right strings to make sure that, should anything happen to her, her youngest son, Sanjay Gandhi, should succeed her. When Sanjay died in a plane crash in 1980, her ambitions were redirected to her eldest son, Rajiv.

Many people, when they face death, attempt to coordinate their *ethos* for after they die. They leave hints and suggestions of what to think of them should the worst happen. Gandhi did exactly this in a speech in Bhubaneswar, capital of Odisha state in eastern India, on 30 October 1984. She said:

> I am here today; I may not be here tomorrow. But the responsibility to look after national interest is on the shoulder of every citizen of India. I have often mentioned this earlier. Nobody knows how many attempts have been made to shoot me, lathis [a stick similar to a baton] have been used to beat me. In Bhubaneswar itself, a brickbat hit me. They have attacked me in every possible manner. I do not care whether I live or die. I have lived a long life and I am proud that I spend the whole of my life in the service of my people. I am only proud of this and nothing else. I shall continue to serve until my last breath and when I die, I can say that every drop of my blood will invigorate India and strengthen it.

This is a powerful expression of *pathos* which built Gandhi's character as one who had devoted her life to the nation. She knew that if she were assassinated, this speech would be remembered and this extract quoted. Gandhi may have been attempting to ensure that in death she was seen as a martyr rather than a tyrant, as well as, perhaps, securing her son's popularity and thus her dynasty.

The following day, on 31 October, Gandhi was assassinated. As she walked past them, her two Sikh bodyguards, Satwant Singh and Beant Singh, fired more than 30 bullets at her. Beant was killed by police fire at the scene of the assassination and Satwant was arrested and later executed. This was the brutal end of Indira Gandhi.

The assassination led to mass anti-Sikh riots across all of India in which an estimated 17,000 Sikh people were murdered, Sikh businesses were smashed up, and countless Sikhs were beaten and raped. Indira Gandhi's rule sowed discord and so did her death. But she secured the fate of her family: her son Ranjay was immediately appointed Prime Minister and her dynasty was secured.

Today, there are mixed feelings about Gandhi. Many still believe she was one of the greatest leaders India ever had. During her time as Prime Minister, she put India on the world map as a major player and a nuclear power. Others look back with a darker view of history. It is never good to compare the dictatorial qualities of different historical figures; however, if one did, we might conclude that Gandhi wasn't as bad as the many men who reigned alongside her. Despite this, due to her actions and the way she wielded power, she is considered to be India's first dictator.

Gandhi is not the only tyrant to have been murdered by her own security. Some 1,941 years earlier, the Roman Emperor Caligula – a notorious psychopath – was killed by his own Praetorian Guard. The Praetorian Guard was made up of elite Roman soldiers who were tasked with protecting the emperor. The history books tell us that Caligula's assassination was led by a guard named Cassius Chaerea, whom Caligula regularly mocked for his high-pitched squeaky voice.

As we can see from both Caligula and Gandhi, being the most powerful person in the nation doesn't necessarily keep you safe from the people closest to you. Indoctrination of the masses doesn't always work. Sometimes all it takes is a few disgruntled individuals nearby with access to weapons.

*Saddam Hussein (1937-2006).
Photo taken in 1998 when Saddam Hussein was about to
deliver a speech on the 10th anniversary of the end of the
Iran-Iraq War.*

16.
SADDAM HUSSEIN

On hearing that his people might not like him, Caligula, the Roman emperor, famously said: 'Let them hate me, as long as they fear me'. Fear has always been an important element of tyranny; however, fear alone is never enough.

It is hard, if not impossible, to truly capture the horrors that Iraqi dictator Saddam Hussein inflicted on his own people. Even his own family were not immune to his terror. Two of his daughters (Rana and Raghad) and their husbands fled Iraq to Jordan in August 1995, claiming that the Iraqi government led by their father was corrupt, incompetent and dangerous. In what appeared to be an act of good faith, Hussein assured them that they had been forgiven for their actions and could return to Iraq in safety and live as ordinary citizens. They decided to believe their patriarch and, in February 1996, returned to Iraq. Both couples were forced to divorce and Hussein's former sons-in-law were denounced as traitors and murdered. In an article for *The Independent*, *Saddam Hussein: The Last Great Tyrant*, Robert Fisk said that Hussein had 'a peculiar ruthlessness, an almost calculated cruelty, perhaps even an interest in pain. It wasn't enough to order the murder of his sons-in-law after their return from exile in Jordan. They had to be dragged away with meat hooks through their eyes'. If Saddam was willing to do this to people who had recently been members of his own family, then no one was safe.

But Hussein did not rule through fear alone. He harvested artificial adoration and paraded it around him wherever he went. To create this lovable *ethos*, Hussein circulated propaganda films of him visiting poor Iraqi families and treating them with kindness. On these televised visits he would often look in their refrigerators and, seeing that they were empty, would have them filled to the brim with food. This made him seem a kind and compassionate leader. He would perform these tokenistic good deeds for the cameras, and then torture people he didn't like when the cameras were turned off, though not always. He balanced a fine line of love and fear. No-one who knew him felt comfortable.

Saddam Hussein's Rise to Power

Hussein rose to power through the Ba'ath Party. The Ba'ath party existed in many Arab countries and believed in Pan-Arabism: the idea that all Arab countries should be unified as one Arab socialist nation.

In 1968, he was involved in a coup which overthrew the Government of Iraq and he became Vice President. During his time as Vice President, he oversaw major economic and political transitions such as the nationalisation of the Western-owned Iraq Petroleum Company. By 1976, as well as being Vice President, Hussein was also a military general. With one foot in the political world and another in the military, he became increasingly popular with Iraqis and his authority began transforming into power: so much power that he was perhaps more influential than the actual President of Iraq, Ahmed Hassan al-Bakr.

In 1979, using al-Bakr's deteriorating health as an excuse, Hussein forced him to resign and became the President of Iraq.

The Purge

The setting is important. Six days after Hussein became President on 16 July 1979, he was seated behind a desk with a row of microphones. In the centre of the raised stage was a standing podium for the speaker. It was vacant. The auditorium was filled with ruling Ba'ath party members who were summoned for a mysterious emergency meeting.

Hussein, while casually puffing on one of his signature cigars, announced that there had been a conspiracy against him and the Ba'ath party. He said:

> The dreams of the conspirators are many. But be assured I will pick up my gun and fight to the end.

Hussein then invited an ally and fellow Ba'ath Party member, Mihyi Abdul-Hussein, to the stage. Showing signs of having been tortured, Abdul-Hussein walked to the stage. He read a speech in which he confessed to taking part in a conspiracy against Saddam Hussein and the Ba'ath Party.

Naturally, this ally was not a traitor, and those words were not his own. Hussein forced him to publicly read that speech by threatening his family. When Saddam Hussein threatened someone's family – which was a common tactic of his – he wouldn't just make the threat. He would have all of the family members rounded up, make his victim stand in front of them while he told them exactly what perverted and depraved things he would have done to them and their family. The threats often involved brutal rape of female relatives including children. Hussein was known to be true to his word. Out of fear for his family's life and honour, Mihyi Abdul-Hussein confessed to a made-up plot.

After Mihyi Abdul-Hussein's confession speech, Hussein stood up and took the podium. Having changed from a seated position to a standing one is a show of seriousness and power. Theatrically giving the stage to the broken Mihyi Abdul-Hussein and then taking it himself demonstrated to everyone in that room that he had complete power.

Now at the podium, after the confession speech, Hussein said:

What means should be used against these traitors?

[PAUSE]

You know the answer. There is no way other than the sword?

[...]

When I have read out your name you shall stand up, recite the party slogan and leave the room.

He began reading names. There were 68 in total. After a name was read out, Hussein stopped speaking and everyone watched as that person was removed from the room by armed men. Some went quietly in shock, some confidently left the room believing that their innocence would keep them safe, others went kicking and screaming – declaring their innocence and love of the Ba'ath party. One man asked why he was being removed. Hussein simply repeated the words: 'When I have read out your name you shall stand up, recite the party slogan and leave the room'. The man did so, and Hussein continued.

All 68 were likely innocent men whom Hussein simply didn't like or saw as a political threat. Out of those 68, 22 were executed later that day. In a sadistic twist which was befitting of Hussein, he ordered the executions to be carried out by the other conspirators whom he decided to spare. His message was clear: *I am in charge. I tell you what to do. I decide who gets to live and who gets to die.* Naturally, all of his political stunts had accompanying speeches. Speeches that were charged with rhetorical mastery and delivered with poetic passion – and broadcast to the entire world.

Domestically – that is to say, excluding his war crimes in other Middle Eastern countries – Saddam Hussein is thought to have been responsible for the deaths of up to 250,000 of his own native Iraqi people. On top of this, the 'Butcher of Baghdad' triggered the Iran-Iraq War, in which more than one million people died. He used chemical weapons against Iraq's minority Kurdish population, whom he systematically persecuted as President. In an act of ruthless revenge, he invaded Kuwait and burnt hundreds of oil wells, destabilising the global economy. The burning of the Kuwaiti oil wells in 1991 is estimated to have destroyed resources which were, at the time, estimated to have cost $157.5 billion USD.

Saddam Hussein's Ethos

How is it possible that the same man who made a point of filling refrigerators could commit such atrocities? It is because Hussein realised that fear alone is not enough to secure true power. Hussein used various forms of propaganda in his attempts to brainwash the

Iraqi people. Some of these, today, seem ridiculous, while others seem downright terrifying.

Hussein, like so many tyrants before him, acted like a deity. At one point, the Iraqi calendar was modified so that the year started on his birthday, 28 April. Similarly to Mobutu, people also sang chants and slogans about Hussein (especially at the start of the new 'new year'). Adults and children alike would chant nonsense such as: 'All Iraq is chanting: Hussein is the glory of our nation'. This ritualistic rote regurgitation of political propaganda works particularly well with younger people and children. If you were 20 years old and all throughout your life you had been told about the glory of your leader, you'd probably end up believing it at some stage. Mass exposure of a rhetorically charged message usually leads to indoctrination.

To reinforce Hussein's image of a glorious leader, his actual image was displayed everywhere. People had his portraits up in their houses, his face was on Iraqi banknotes, and, when the internet and computers began to take off, all government officials were ordered to have a picture of Hussein as their screensaver. His friendly face was on highway billboards, in school classrooms, and on the entrances of public buildings – everyone knew who he was, and everyone understood that they were expected to be grateful.

The War Speech

In extreme cases, usually towards the end of their reigns when they are slowly losing control, tyrants and dictators resort to giving speeches for survival.

In Saddam Hussein's case, he had upset nations more powerful than his own and faced a full-scale invasion from the United States of America and a number of its close allies. Facing the possible elimination of his reign, Hussein went on to give speeches encouraging his people to remain loyal and fight to the death.

When the cracks in a dictatorial regime begin to show, many dictators invoke the authority of a higher power: God. Generally speaking, the more desperate a situation is, the more a tyrant talks about God. Faith is a very emotive subject: it can motivate people to march to their deaths and achieve remarkable feats. Whether it was fear or faith, Hussein was no doubt aware of the powers that *pathos* had in controlling his people.

On 24 March 2003, five days into the invasion of Iraq, Hussein gave a speech that was broadcast on Iraqi national television. He said:

> Now we are living through decisive days in which fighters and the great Iraqi people are doing exceptionally well and for which they deserve victory and satisfaction from God – as He promised the true faithful against the enemies of God and humanity.
>
> It is our right, nay our duty, to be proud as fighting believers who are patient in this epic war...
>
> We have always complied, even with what is illegitimate and unjust among the demands and allegations of the evil ones, in the hope that the world would awake and lift the sanctions against our people and so that we avoid the evils of war.
>
> And after they ran out of excuses or cover, the invading aggressors came openly and shamelessly with vicious intent as we know them and their intentions to be.

As well as the strong *argumentum ad hominem* against the explicitly-stated 'evil ones', Hussein used a lot of religious language to spur the emotions of his zealous audience. The application of *pathos* was used to convince his people to keep following him even though the nation was falling to pieces. It is hard for an indoctrinated audience to resist the call of their dictator invoking the power of the divine.

An interesting point to observe in this speech is the use of *aporia* when Hussein said: 'It is our right, nay our duty'. It is unlikely that Hussein spontaneously corrected himself in the middle of a televised speech. As we have seen, *Aporia* is a rhetorical technique when a speaker corrects themselves or expresses a doubt over what they are saying or will say next. The effect of *aporia* is that it makes what is being said sound more authentic – as if it is spontaneous rather than scripted. Hussein would have no doubt scripted that correction to make his speech seem more spontaneous and thus authentic. Such displays of seeming authenticity are designed to hook an audience's engagement and win over their trust.

The use of the adjective 'epic' to describe the war could be interpreted as a use of *kairos*, as he was invoking the momentousness of an occasion to boost its gravity.

Hussein went on to say:

> O brothers, you know that our country's policy is to avoid evil. But when evil comes, armed with deceit and destruction, we must face them with faith and holy struggle in a manner which dignifies us and satisfies God.
>
> And here you are today standing, o valiant Iraqis, glorious women and brave armed forces, in a manner which pleases friends and the faithful and enrages the enemies and infidels. A stand which will make you victorious, God willing, against your enemies...

The idea that Iraq under Hussein's rule had a policy to 'avoid evil' is a lie; nevertheless, he said it to emphasise the binary trope of good and evil: the holy vs the unholy. Hussein used the *antithesis* of 'deceit and destruction' of the enemy against the 'faith and holy struggle' of the Iraqi people to emphasise the *false dichotomy* (a binary opposite which presents no option for middle ground) he was presenting to the Iraqi people.

Saddam Hussein knew that, to meet his objective of motivating the Iraqi people to fight, he must get them to rally their support with more than just fear (after all, many of them would have more fear for the invading forces). So, Hussein took the textbook move of flattery and used *comprobatio*. We can see this when he used the *tricolon* of adjectives: 'valiant' 'glorious' and 'brave' – also *abundantia*. Hussein knew that to win this war his people needed to believe that they were those things, and they needed to believe that they had a leader worth fighting for – one that saw their worth.

Another example of *kairos* can be seen when Hussein said, 'and you are today standing'. His audience were well aware that they were standing that day; but by reminding them, Hussein signalled to each and every Iraqi watching that they were present for that war and that they each had a role to fulfil if they wanted to see victory.

After having adequately worked up his audience by invoking the command of time and God, Hussein gave them express directions: a violent call to action.

In President Hussein's own words:

> O brave fighters, hit your enemy with all your strength. O Iraqis, fight with the strength of the spirit of jihad which you carry in you and push them to the point where they cannot go on.

In this extract, Hussein called on both the soldiers and all Iraqis to fight against the US-led invasion. After years of living under Hussein's tyranny, the Iraqi people knew never to refuse an order. Especially when the order was directed at you. One of the ways Hussein directed the action to specific people was through the direct address and the way he changed who he was addressing with *apostrophe*. Hussein spoke first to the fighters, then to all Iraqis. This subtle change of addressee signaled the universality of the order, and thus reinforced his message.

Hussein's speech sent a clear message: all God-fearing (and Saddam-fearing) people needed to rally and fight to ward off the 'evil ones'. He closed his speech by repeating and reinforcing his call to action:

> Hit them so that good and its people may reign and evil evicted back to its place. Mothers, daughters, fathers and sons, together with all the faithful and good, will sleep in comfort after being terrified by aggression. Your struggle will dishearten the aggressor. Oh Arabs, oh faithful of the world, oh those who support justice and oppose evil, we herald the victory that God has promised us in the conflict against the lowlifes and enemies of humanity.

Once more he presented his audience with the *antithesis* between the personified 'good' and the 'evil' that needed eviction. He closed his speech by listing the people he was addressing, 'Mothers, daughters, fathers and sons'; thus, emphasising the emotive family links to which each person can connect, through both *pathos* and *abundantia*.

This addressing of the audience continued when he used the *anaphoric tricolon*, 'Oh Arabs [...] oh faithful [...] oh those who support justice and oppose evil'. By listing his audience, he was further enhancing his use of *pathos*: the Iraqi listeners on whom his reign depended were more likely to feel seen, to feel accepted, to feel empowered.

Finally, to close his speech, Hussein went back to God and a little more *ad hominem* hatred for the enemy when he said: 'We herald the victory that God has promised us in the conflict against the lowlifes and enemies of humanity'.

It was a riling speech, a hypocritical condemnation of violence, and a passionate call for war. Hussein pulled all the tricks in the book to get his audience on his side. In many ways, it was a good effort. But he was probably doomed the moment the US invaded.

Conclusion of Saddam Hussein

Saddam Hussein wanted to be feared, but he also wanted to be admired. He attempted to straddle both, and define his *ethos* in a way that would allow him to keep his people in line: a line that he could exploit, beat up, praise, and command. For 24 long years he got away with it.

But despite his best efforts, Hussein lost the war and was forced into hiding. On 13 December 2003, US soldiers found Hussein hiding in a dingy hole in the ground underneath a rock. The moments after his discovery were televised and shared in the media. A bearded and broken-looking Hussein was inspected by US troops before being handed over to the authorities of the newly-formed Iraqi government. Long gone was the *ethos* of the powerful tyrant.

Hussein was put on trial, which was partly televised. He was seen making threatening gestures while witnesses were giving testimony of torture and abuse, leading people to suspect that it was a signal to attack the witness' family. The trial found Saddam Hussein guilty of multiple counts of crimes against humanity, and sentenced him to death.

On 30 December 2006, Saddam Hussein was executed by hanging, his request for a firing squad having been denied. An official video released by the Iraqi government showed him walking to the gallows, and having the rope placed on his neck, where the video was then cut. The execution was not meant to be seen by anyone apart from the people who were invited to watch it live. However, one of the people present secretly recorded it on their phone, and the clip went viral. In it, Sadam was jeered and argued with the people who were heckling him. He attempted to recite the Islamic Shahada, but the trap door was opened before he could finish.

Like the mad emperor Caligula, Indira Gandhi, and so many leaders throughout history, Hussein, the Butcher of Baghdad, was killed by his own people.

It would be wrong to conclude this chapter without mentioning that the rhetoric of war is used by both sides, the evil and the righteous. As an example, in 2005, when people were beginning to question the nature of the American invasion, US President George W Bush shared an anecdote about his little chat with God. He said:

> I am driven with a mission from God. God would tell me: 'George go and fight these terrorists in Afghanistan'. And I did. Then God would tell me, 'George, go and end the tyranny in Iraq'. And I did.

The *anaphoric* repetition and 'And I did' adds a slightly eerie undertone to this justification delivered by Bush to the American people; however, the message was clear: *I did the righteous work of God.*

So said many others...

CONCLUSION

If there is one thing that I want you to take from this book it is that no matter where you look in history, no matter what corner of the earth, no matter what language or culture, the worst people of that age – the tyrants, the dictators and their cronies – will probably be saying variations of the same things in the same ways.

History is full of variation; however, the rule of rhetoric remains mostly unchanged. For example, invoking religion to create *ethos* can be seen in the speeches of both Julius Caesar and Saddam Hussein. Despite worshipping different gods and coming from completely alternate worlds, they both invoked religion to justify policy decisions.

Another example is how *argumentum ad hominem* is used to create either fear or bravery. Napoleon and Attila the Hun used *argumentum ad hominem* to build bravery in their troops, while Eva Perón and Jiang Qing used it to vilify a mysterious hidden enemy that the audience should fear and rise against.

One of the most interesting observations is how rhetoric seems to transcend culture. Even the isolationist Queen Ranavalona I of

Madagascar used variations of fear-mongering and ethos. As did Wu Zetian, who would have also had little exposure to Western speeches.

While a ruler may have a very distinct *ethos*, they never have only one. Chinggis Khan was a mighty dreadful warrior, but he was also a kind, supportive friend. In the same way Napoleon was the glorious emperor in one speech, and the angry general in another. *Ethos* is a complicated philosophical challenge that we all face. That is why carved onto the Temple of Apollo in Delphi are the words 'know thyself' – if it was a straightforward thing to do the Ancient Greeks wouldn't have carved it into stone at one of their holiest sites.

Rhetoric has a very strong relationship with war. War requires the utmost sacrifice and the emotive features of rhetoric can convince people – both civilians and soldiers – to sacrifice their lives and their livelihoods. Rulers often invoke natural imagery to comfort people with the concept of death and to embolden them with the prospects of victory. For example, both Chinggis Khan and Napoleon used imagery of water. Goebbels invoked the power of a storm. To add to the use of imagery, the rhetorical feature of contrast (*antithesis*) is also incredibly powerful in giving people a wider perspective, showing that their own life is of little consequence, but what they are fighting for is worth any sacrifice. And to complement both of these features flattery is universal: which is why *comprobatio* is used in wars to empower and embolden the people making the sacrifices.

The most dangerous feature of rhetoric (more so than merely encouraging people to die) is that it can manipulate an audience into believing that they are on the side of 'good'. Rhetoric can cripple reasoning. When an audience sees a narrative of good and bad, they are empowered to destroy the bad, and that has often meant committing atrocities.

Each tyrant featured in this book had one thing in common: they had mastered at least one element of rhetoric and often several. They each understood the power of the spoken word and used that power of their own nefarious purposes.

Even the mighty men whom history has glorified in popular culture for their violence, the warriors and barbarians of the past, gave eloquent heartfelt speeches to their friends and soldiers. Even the women, whom modern historians have predominantly sidelined, sometimes as wives and sometimes as rulers in their own right, gave rousing battle speeches, mighty edicts, and logically twisted addresses to break democracies, twist ideologies, and shatter the spirits of their foes.

What messages should we take from this rhetorical exploration into the words of malice? It is that words are more powerful than most people realise. They dictate elements of our lives, often without us noticing, and, despite their impact on history over the years, these rhetorical tools are still being used for nefarious purposes today. And, as was the case throughout most of history, the masses are still falling for their tricks.

So, is rhetoric evil? In the same way that a wall is neither good nor evil, rhetoric is neither good nor evil. It is the intention with which rhetoric is used that should define our ethical judgement. While rhetoric is often the tool of tyranny, it is important to remember that it is also used by those that history has classified as 'good'. We can look at vilified people throughout history and accuse them of being rhetoric-wielding monsters, but the same tropes are used by those whom history has chosen to glorify: the good and the righteous. Rhetoric is influence. Influence is power. And power can be both good or evil.

Despite being akin to a double-edged sword, there is no denying that the abuse of rhetoric has wreaked havoc on humanity throughout history on many occasions. Despite the many lessons of history, we still live in a world with tyranny: a world with war, corruption, and persecution. The rhetorical lessons from the past are as relevant today as they have ever been. Indeed, we are living in an age that some have deemed to be an age of post-truth. An age where simplified messages overpower sophisticated ones – an age where the art of debate is dying and most discourse has devolved into oversimplified binary positions to which ordinary people are expected to pledge their allegiance. Some go as far as to claim that populist rhetoric, propagated through new social media platforms, is once more rearing its ugly head. The case can be made that rhetoric today is just as scary, just as powerful, and just as relevant as it has been throughout history.

If you listen closely, you will still hear echoes of the language of evil.

GLOSSARY OF RHETORICAL TERMS

abundantia (*a-bund-dan-ti-a*) – derives from the Latin word *abundo* meaning 'exceed'. *Abundantia* is when many words meaning the same thing are used to create an all-encompassing effect.

anadiplosis (*a-nuh-dip-low-sis*) – derives from the Greek word *dipoles* meaning 'double' and the prefix *ana* meaning 'backwards'. *Anadiplosis* is when a word at the beginning of a clause is repeated at the beginning of the next.

anaphora (*ah-nah-fuh-rah*) – a Latin word from the original Greek, meaning 'repetition'. *Ana* – means 'back' and *pherein* 'to bear'. *Anaphora* is repetition at the end of a sentence, paragraph or clause.

antithesis (*an-it-thuh-suhs*) – a Latin word from the original Greek meaning 'placed against'. *Anti* means 'against' and *tithenai* means 'to place'. So *antithesis* is when something is placed against something else – a meaningful contrast which is constructed for effect.

aporia (*ah-por-ee-yah*) – derives from the Greek meaning 'impassable'. In rhetoric, *aporia* refers to when a speaker pretends to be uncertain about what they are saying.

apostrophe (*ah-po-struh-fee*) – a Greek word meaning 'turning away.' In speech, apostrophe refers to when a speaker breaks away from their audience to address someone else.

argumentum ad hominem (*ad hom-in-em*) – a Latin phrase meaning 'to argue to the person'. *Argumentum* comes from the Latin *aruguere* meaning 'to make clear.' *Ad* literally translates to 'to.' *Hominem* is the Latin for 'man'. *Argumentum ad hominem* is when a speaker attempts to criticise an argument by criticising the person (or organisation) delivering it.

argumentum ad populum (*ad pop-u-lum*) – a Latin phrase meaning to argue through the masses. *Argumentum* comes from the Latin *aruguere* meaning 'to make clear.' *Ad* literally translates to 'to.' *Populum* is the Latin accusative singular of *populus* meaning 'people'. *Argumentum ad populum* is when a speaker attempts to grant an argument legitimacy based on support from the people.

argumentum ad rem (*ad rem*) – a Latin phrase meaning to argue to the matter. *Argumentum* comes from the Latin *aruguere* meaning 'to make clear.' *Ad* literally translates to 'to.' *Rem* is the Latin accusative of *res* which means 'matter'. *Argumentum ad rem* is when you criticise an argument by attacking its logic (or the substance).

chiasmus (*key-as-mus*) – a Latin word originating from the Greek letter *chi* (Χχ) which used to mean a crossover arrangement. In rhetoric, a *chiasmus* is when there is repetition in an ABBA pattern.

comprobatio (*kum-pro-ba-tio*) – a Latin word meaning 'full approval.' In rhetoric, *comprobatio* is when you approve a future in the audience (usually to win their favour).

elenchus (*el-ench-us*) – a Latin word from the Greek word *elenkhos*, meaning 'scrutiny.' *Elenchus* is when a series of questions are used to prove a point through a logical progression.

enargia (*e-nar-ge-a*) – an Ancient Greek word deriving from 'argos' which means 'bright'. In rhetoric, *enargia* refers to a vivid or bright description.

enthymeme (*ent-thee-mee-m*) – an *enthymeme* is when you have a logical syllogism with an implied premise or conclusion. It derives from the Greek words *en* meaning 'within' and *thumos* meaning 'mind.'

epiplexis (*eh-pee-plex-us*) – a Greek word meaning 'to rebuke'. *Epiplexis* is a rhetorical question which is designed to rebuke.

epistrophe (*ep-ist-rof-ee*) – a Greek word meaning 'to turn around.' *Epi* means to turn around and *strephein* means 'to turn.' So *epistrophe* is when the same word or phrase returns at the end of each sentence, paragraph or clause.

epizeuxis (*epi-zuk-sis*) – a Greek word meaning 'to join together'. *Epizeuxis* is when a word is repeated in immediate consecutive order for effect.

erotema (*ay-ro-tay-ma*) – a Greek word meaning 'question'. In rhetorical terms is exclusively a question which does not require a response (a rhetorical question).

ethos (*eh-thos*) – a Greek word meaning 'nature/disposition'. *Ethos* is how a person or organisation chooses to characterise themselves.

isocolon (*ayh-suh-koh-lon*) – an Ancient Greek word meaning 'equal parts'. *Isos* is the Greek for 'equal' and *colon* means 'parts'. In rhetoric, an *isocolon* is when there are sentences or clauses of a repeated equal length to create effect.

kairos (*kai-ros*) – a Greek word meaning 'opportune moment'. In rhetoric, *kairos* is when someone references time or the opportune moment to deliver a message.

logos (*loh-gos*) – a Greek word meaning 'reason'. In rhetoric it is used to refer to logic used for persuasion.

occultatio (*oh-kul-ta-tee-oh*) – derives from the Latin word *occulo* meaning 'to conceal'. Occultatio is when you say something by saying that you are not going to say it.

pathos (*pay-thos*) – from the original Greek word pathos which means 'suffering'. *Pathos* later came to mean any application of emotive language beyond just suffering.

syllogism (*si-luh-ji-zm*) – a syllogism is a logical structure. The word originates from the Greek words *syn* meaning 'with' and *logizesthai* meaning 'reason' (which itself comes from the Greek word logos).

tricolon (*tri-ko-lon*) – a Greek word meaning 'three parts'.
Tri means 'three' and *colon* means 'parts'. In the case of rhetoric, *colon* means a sentence or clause which is grammatically – although not necessarily logically – complete. In rhetoric, a *tricolon* refers to when something is structured into three parts.

LIST OF ILLUSTRATIONS

Image 1: Julius Caesar (100 BC-44 BC). Portrait by Peter Paul Rubens, oil on panel, c.1625/6. Picture credit: IanDagnall Computing/Alamy Stock Photo. Page: 16

Image 2: Attila the Hun (c 406-453) as shown in the Nuremberg Chronicle in 1493. Picture credit: Pictorial Press Ltd / Alamy Stock Photo. Page: 28

Image 3: Wu Zetian (624-05) as depicted in an 18th-century album of portraits of 86 emperors of China, with Chinese historical notes. Originally published/produced in China, 18th century. (British Library, Shelfmark Or. 2231) Picture Credit: Wikipedia Commons. Page: 40

Image 4: Genghis Khan[a] (c. 1162-1227). Reproduction of a 1278 portrait paint and ink on silk taken from a Yuan-era album – National

Palace Museum, Taipei. Picture Credit: Wikipedia Commons. Page: 50

Image 5: Isabella of Castile (1451-1504). Anonymous portrait of Isabella I, c.1490. Picture Credit: Wikipedia Commons. Page: 64

Image 6: Mary I (1516-1558). Portrait by Antonis Mor, 1554 in The Yorck Project (2002). Picture Credit: The Yorck Project (2002) /Wikipedia Commons. Page: 70

Image 7: Elizabeth I (1533-1603). The Darnley Portrait, c.1575, was named after a previous owner. The author of the painting is unknown. Picture Credit: Wikipedia Commons. Page: 76

Image 8: Napoleon Bonaparte (1769-1821). The Emperor Napoleon crossing the Alps, 1800 by Jacques-Louis David. Picture Credit: Wikipedia Commons. Page: 82

Image 9: Ranavalona I (1778-1861). Philippe-Auguste Ramanankirahina (1860-1915) - Photograph of the original work displayed at the Lapan' Andafiavaratra (Antananarivo). Picture Credit: PublicDomain/ Wikipedia Commons. Page: 96

Image 10: Benito Mussolini (1883-1945). Portrait printed in the Italian magazine Tempoin 1939. Picture Credit: Wikipedia Commons. Page: 108

Image 11: Paul Joseph Goebbels (1897-1945). Portrait taken in 1933 by photographer Heinrich Hoffmann. Picture Credit: Heinrich Hoffmann/Wikipedia Commons. Page: 124

Image 12: Adolf Hitler (1889-1945). Official portrait taken in 1938 by Heinrich Hoffmann. Picture Credit: Heinrich Hoffmann/Wikipedia Commons. Page: 140

Image 13: Joseph Stalin (1878-1953). Picture of Stalin at the Tehran Conference, 1943. Picture Credit: Franklin D. Roosevelt Library Public Domain Photographs/Wikipedia Commons. Page: 154

Image 14: Eva Péron (1919-1952). Picture of Eva Péron taken by photographer Pinélides Aristóbulo Fusco in 1948. Picture Credit: Pinélides Aristóbulo Fusco/Wikipedia Commons. Page: 166

Image 15: Jiang Qing (1914-1991). Photograph taken in 1976 by an unknown author. Picture Credit: Wikipedia Commons. Page: 178

Image 16: Mobutu Sese Seko (1930-1997). Photograph taken in 1983 by Frank Hall as President Mobutu met with U.S. Secretary of Defense Caspar W. Weinberger in his Pentagon office, Room 3E880. Picture Credit: Frank Hall/Wikipedia Commons. Page: 192

Image 17: Indira Gandhi (1917-1984). Official portrait taken in 1983. Picture Credit: Wikipedia Commons. Page: 204

Image 18: Saddam Hussein (1937-2006). Photo taken in 1998 when Saddam Hussein was about to deliver a speech on the 10th anniversary of the end of the Iran-Iraq War. Picture Credit: Wikipedia Commons. Page: 216

INDEX

A

abundantia 237, 54, 61, 86, 88, 162, 211, 224, 226
Adolf Eichmann 168
Alexander the Great 71
Anadiplosis 88, 237
anaphora 237, 22, 24, 25, 37, 42, 79, 90, 117, 120, 147, 148, 170, 171, 199, 211
  anaphoric 53, 59, 88, 93, 99, 148, 161, 162, 170, 211, 226, 228
anecdote 92, 114
Anne Boleyn 71, 72
Anne of Cleves 71
antithesis 237, 22, 25, 38, 46, 59, 61, 78, 79, 101, 116, 118, 133, 146, 162, 186, 198, 208, 224, 226
antithesis of enargeia 59
apodioxis 238
Aporia 158, 223
apostrophe 238
  88, 158, 225
Argentina 167, 168, 169, 170, 174, 176
  Buenos Aires 168, 169
arguments 238, 239, 241
argumentum ad hominem 238, 35, 45, 74, 86, 87, 118, 120, 127, 137, 144, 145, 146, 151, 158, 162, 183, 186, 187, 198, 200, 201, 206, 223
Argumentum ad populum 120, 134

Argumentum ad rem 144
Attila the Hun 28, 29, 30, 31, 32, 33, 34, 35, 36, 37, 38, 39, 45, 46, 53, 54, 55, 57, 73, 75, 78, 86, 134, 198
  Alani 35, 36

B

Ba'ath Party
  218, 219
Battle of Catalaunian Plains
  32
Belgium 17, 193, 194
Bleda 30, 31 ·
British Empire 55, 84, 91

C

Caligula 24, 213, 214, 217, 227
Catherine Howard 71
Catherine of Aragon 71
Catholicism 66, 72
  Catholic 66, 69, 71, 72, 77, 79, 80
Chiasmus 173
China 40, 41, 44, 48, 54, 55, 179, 180, 181, 183, 184, 185, 190, 208
  Chinese 40, 41, 44, 180, 181, 185, 186, 188, 189

Chinese Civil War 180
Chinese Red Army 180
Chinggis Khan 10, 27, 39, 51, 52, 54, 55, 56, 57, 58, 59, 60, 61, 62, 68, 84, 85, 86, 89, 99, 133, 134
  Börte 52, 54
  Father Munglig 57, 58
  Jamuqa 53, 54
  Jelme 59, 60
  Jin dynasty 55
  Khubilai 59, 60
  Merkits 52, 53, 54
  Mongolia 51, 52
  Mongolian Tugrik 52
  Mongols 39, 52, 53, 54, 55, 56, 57
  Munglig 57, 58, 59, 60
  Subetei 59, 60
  Tartars 56
  Temüjin 51, 52, 53, 54
  the Mongol empire 52
  The Secret History of the Mongols 52, 55, 56
  To'otil Qan 54
  Western Xia Empire 55
  Xi Xia 62
  Zhongdu 55
Christianity 101, 104
Cicero 11, 17, 18, 19
communism 180, 181, 182, 187, 195
comprobatio 239
  32, 33, 46, 57, 61, 73, 86, 99, 171, 182, 224
concessio 157, 158
conclusion 239
Congo 193, 194, 195, 196, 197, 202

D

Danube 31
Dennis Globe 125
  The Art of Great Speeches 125

digressio 239
direct address 68, 73

E

Eastern Roman Empire 31
Egypt 17
elenchus 239
  103, 104
Emperor 32, 42, 43, 44, 45, 46, 47
emphasis 85, 93, 104
enargia 37, 198
England 71, 72, 73, 74, 77, 79, 80, 101, 148, 149, 151, 152
enthymeme 239
epiplexis 103, 239
epistrophe 240 42, 93, 103, 162, 182, 211
epizeuxis 240
erotema 34
ethics 141, 146
ethos 240, 20, 21, 22, 24, 25, 26, 27, 29, 35, 38, 39, 46, 67, 73, 74, 79, 89, 91, 98, 99, 101, 103, 105, 116, 117, 120, 121, 155, 156, 157, 158, 160, 170, 171, 181, 182, 183, 186, 187, 190, 196, 197, 198, 199, 202, 206, 207, 212, 218, 221, 226
Europe 55
Eva Perón 167, 169, 172, 175, 176, 184, 202
  Juan Perón 167, 168, 174
    Peronism 167, 172
    Secretary of Labour and Social Welfare 168
  La Razón de mi vida 176
  Loyalty Day 168, 169
  Perón 167, 168, 169, 170, 171, 172, 173, 174, 175, 176, 184, 202

F

false dichotomy 118, 200, 224
fascism 110
  fascist 110, 111, 112, 114, 123
  Fascists 113, 114
Flagellum Dei
  31, 38
Flattery 46
France 17, 32, 83, 84, 85, 86, 87, 91, 92, 93, 94, 97
Francis Bacon 12
  English philosopher 12

G

genetic fallacy 74
George Bush Jr 21
  US President 21
Germany 9, 125, 126, 127, 128, 129, 130, 138, 142, 143, 145, 146, 147, 148, 149, 151, 152, 156, 157, 158, 160, 161, 162, 163, 168
  German 9, 14, 122, 126, 128, 129, 130, 131, 132, 135, 136, 142, 143, 144, 145, 146, 147, 148, 152, 156, 157, 158, 159, 160, 161, 162, 163
  German 6th Army 129
Greek 237, 238, 239, 240, 241
Greek philosopher Aristotle 11
Greeks 52

H

havoc 9
Hitler 10, 13, 14, 125, 126, 127, 128, 129, 130, 135, 138, 140, 141, 142, 143, 144, 145, 146, 147, 148, 149, 150, 151, 152, 153, 156, 161, 162, 163
  Brownshirts 142
  Enabling Act of 1933 143
  Iron Cross 142
  Mein Kampf 125, 142
  Nazism 14
    Nazis 14, 33, 122, 125, 129, 130, 134, 135, 136, 137, 138, 144, 153, 156, 168, 184
  The Reichstag 143
  the Weimar 143
Holocaust 144, 168
Hungary 30
Hunnic 30, 31
Huns 29, 31, 35, 37, 38, 55
hyperbole 59
  hyperbolic 60, 136
hypophora 240

I

imagery 36, 38, 46, 55, 56, 59, 60, 90, 122, 136, 198
implied premise 239
India 205, 206, 207, 208, 209, 210, 211, 212, 213
Indira Gandhi 204, 205, 213, 227
  Golden Temple 210, 212
  High Court 112, 113, 205
  Indian Parliament 205
  Janata coalition 209, 210
  Jawaharlal Nehru 207
  Operation Bluestar 210
  Sikh 210, 211, 212, 213
Iraq 21, 216, 217, 218, 221, 222, 224, 227
Isabella of Castile 64, 65, 71
  Christopher Columbus 68

Inquisition 65, 66
Isabella 27, 64, 65, 66, 67, 68, 69, 71, 72, 73, 77
Marquis 67, 68
Portuguese War 67
Sabbath 66
Spanish Catholics 66
Spanish Inquisition 65, 66
Spanish Queen Isabella of Castile 65
Tomás de Torquemada 66
Yom Kippur 66

isocolon 53, 120, 133, 134, 149, 240
Italy 84, 85, 88, 109, 111, 112, 113, 114, 115, 116, 117, 118, 119, 120, 121, 122

J

Jane Seymour 71
Japan 145, 180
   Japanese 180, 183, 184, 185, 186, 187, 188, 189
Jean-Paul Sartre 135
Jerusalem 47
Jews 65, 66, 69, 135, 136, 142, 144, 145, 146, 147, 149, 150, 151, 152
   Jewish 66, 127, 128, 130, 135, 142, 143, 144, 145, 146, 147, 148, 149, 150, 151, 152, 153, 168
Jiang Qing 178, 179, 180, 181, 182, 184, 186, 187, 189, 190
   Chairman Mao 179, 180, 182, 183, 188, 190
      Mao 179, 180, 181, 182, 183, 188, 189, 190
   Cultural Revolution 180, 181, 189
   Gang of Four 180
   Great Proletarian Cultural Revolution 180
   Jiang 178, 179, 180, 181, 182, 183, 184, 185, 186, 187, 189, 190
   Legend of the Red Lantern 184, 185, 187, 189
   Politburo 181
John Foxe 72
   Book of Martyrs 72
Jonathan Clements 42
Jordanes 32, 38, 39
Joseph Goebbels 9, 124, 125, 127, 246
   Anka Stalherm 128
   Battle of Stalingrad 129, 156
   Else Janke 128
   Minister of Propaganda 9
   Minister of Public Enlightenment and Propaganda 128
   Nazi Germany 9
   Soviet Red Army 129
   Sportpalast 130
   Total War speech 129, 130, 131, 134, 135
   University of Heidelberg 127
Joseph Mengele 168
Joseph Stalin 129, 154, 155, 163
   Ioseb Besarionis dze Jughashvili 155
   Kuntsevo Dacha 163
   Man of Steel 155
   Red Army Parade 156
   Tsar Nicholas II 155
   Yakov Dzhugashvili 156
Julie Mell 150
   The Myth of the Medieval Jewish Moneylender 150
Julius Caesar 9, 10, 16, 17, 19, 20, 21, 22, 25, 47, 89, 199, 245
   Battle of Zela 23
   Caligula 24
   Dictator 17
   Gallic Wars 25
   Gaul 25, 26
   Gnaeus Domitius Calvinus 23
   Latin 18, 22, 23, 24, 25
   lawyer 17
   Life of Caesar 19
      Plutarch 19, 23
   Pharnaces II 23
   politician 17, 19, 23
   Pompey 20

Pontus 23
Rhodes 19
river Rubicon 20
Roman Republic 19
Rome 17, 19, 20, 23, 27
Senate 20
Suetonius 18, 19, 20

K

kairos 33, 53, 75, 89, 90, 105, 116, 120, 121, 134, 137, 146, 157, 160, 161, 162, 173, 186, 223, 224, 240
Katherine Parr 71
King Henry VIII 71, 74
Korea 55

L

Latin 237, 238, 239, 241, 242
Lenin 155, 156, 159
letter 239
logic 239, 241, 242
  logical structure 241
logical fallacies 149
logical syllogism 21, 74
logos 20, 21, 22, 25, 74, 117, 121, 144, 145, 146, 162, 182, 207, 240, 241

M

Madagascar 10, 97, 98, 99, 101, 106, 107
Mark Antony 9
metaphor 9, 60, 85, 86, 132, 146, 158, 172, 174, 179, 183, 187, 198

Michael Schatzberg 197
  The Dialects of Oppression in Zaire 196
Mobutu 192, 193, 195, 196, 197, 198, 199, 200, 201, 202, 221
  Congo Crisis 195, 196
  Joseph-Désiré Mobutu 195, 197
  Lumumba 193, 194, 195, 196
  Mama Yemo 199
  Papa Mobutu 196, 197, 200
  Rwandan Genocide 202
Mussolini 108, 109, 110, 111, 112, 113, 114, 115, 116, 117, 118, 119, 120, 121, 122, 123, 142, 167
  Abyssinia 115, 119, 120, 121
  Blackshirts 110, 111, 113, 115, 116, 142
  fascist political ideology 110
  Giacomo Matteotti 112, 114
    Matteotti 112, 114
  Grand Council 122
  League of Nations 119, 120
  Luigi Facta 111
  National Fascist Party 110
  Prime Minister 99, 111, 112
  Victor Emmanuel III 111, 113, 122

N

Napoleon 27, 34, 82, 83, 84, 85, 86, 87, 88, 89, 90, 91, 92, 93, 94, 97, 99, 134, 141, 159, 179
  Corsica 84
  Emperor of France 83, 93
  Holy Roman Empire 85, 87
  Imperial French Princess 83
  King of Holland 83
  King of Naples 83
  King of Spain 72, 77, 83
  King of Westphalia 83
  Mantua 87, 89
  Mediterranean island of Elba 92
  Napoleon Bonaparte 82, 83

Napoleonic Wars 89, 93
Pope Pius VII 83
Seventh Coalition 93
the Battle of Toulon 84
the Battle of Waterloo 93
The Third Coalition 89
War of the Third Coalition 89

Nazis 14

Nazism 14
  antisemitic 128, 142, 147, 149, 150, 152
  historical crime 14
  Nazi 9, 122, 125, 126, 127, 128, 129, 130, 135, 137, 143, 145, 149, 152, 156, 167, 168
  Nazi party 125, 126, 128, 143
  Nazi regime 125, 135, 152
  Third Reich 126

O

Occultatio 171

oxymoron 172

P

paronomasia 241

pathos 20, 22, 25, 36, 39, 53, 56, 57, 60, 61, 62, 86, 87, 89, 104, 114, 116, 117, 132, 137, 148, 170, 171, 172, 175, 186, 189, 207, 208, 213, 222, 223, 226, 241

Patriotism 208

Periphrasis 241

Phiasel Tower 47

phrase 238, 240, 241

Pope Leo I 39

Praetorian Guard 213

Priscus 29, 30

propaganda speeches 126

Protestantism 71, 72
  Protestant 71, 72, 79
  Protestants 72

Q

Queen Elizabeth I 65, 77, 80
  James VI 80
  Princess Elizabeth 72, 75, 77
  the Spanish Armada 77, 80
  The Tilbury Speech 77

Queen Isabella I of Spain 27

Queen Mary I 65, 71
  Bloody Mary 71, 75, 77
  Edward VI 72
  Guildhall Speech 72
  Henry VIII 71, 72, 74, 77
  King Philip II 74
  Mary 65, 70, 71, 72, 73, 74, 75, 77, 78, 79, 80
  Mary I 65, 70, 71, 72, 73, 75, 77, 134
  Pope 39, 71
  Princess Elizabeth 72, 75, 77
  Tower of London 75, 77
  Wyatt Rebellion 72, 73

R

Ranavalona I 10, 96, 97, 98, 101, 103, 106, 107
  Ambaninandro 99, 100
  King Radama I 98
  Rakotobe 98
  The Coronation Speech 98

reductio ad absurdum 241

repetition 237, 239

rhetoric 9, 10, 11, 12, 13, 14
  art of deceit 11
  art of persuasion 10

pattern of repetition 10
rhetorical patterns 10
rhetorical questions 34, 38, 100, 103, 104, 118
rhetoric of dictatorship 9
rhythm 18, 22, 24, 53, 117, 121, 132, 134, 170
Robert Fisk 217
Roman Empire 29, 31, 32
Roman Gaul 32
Romans 24, 31, 47, 52, 55
Roman statesman and lawyer Cicero 11
Rome 17, 19, 20, 23, 27, 71, 91, 92, 111
Royal families of the Continent 91
Russia 37, 89, 91, 155, 160, 161

S

Saddam Hussein 216, 217, 218, 219, 221, 222, 224, 226, 227
  Ahmed Hassan al-Bakr 218
  Mihyi Abdul-Hussein 219
sentence 237, 240, 241
Serdica 31
Shakespeare 9, 11, 103, 152
  King Lear 11
  Merchant of Venice 103, 152
    Shylock 103, 152
short sentences 121, 131, 132, 160
  short simple sentences 131, 137
Spain 17, 27, 66, 72, 74, 77, 79
  Segovia 67, 68, 73
speech 9, 12, 13, 14, 18, 26, 27
St Peter 39
syllogisms 239, 241

T

Theodoric I 32, 39
Theodosius II 31
tricolon 22, 24, 25, 26, 35, 42, 79, 80, 87, 88, 90, 93, 99, 104, 113, 116, 117, 118, 136, 147, 148, 162, 163, 170, 171, 182, 187, 199, 211, 224, 226, 241, 242
Tsars of Russia 91
tu quoque 242
tyrants 10

U

Union of Soviet Socialist Republics 155
  Soviet 129, 155, 156, 163, 183, 184, 195
  USSR 155, 156, 157, 158, 160, 161, 163

V

Valentinian III 32
Vatican 39
Vienna 85, 92, 141
Visigoths 31, 32, 35, 36

W

war 9, 10, 20, 26, 27
  civil war 20, 27
Western Roman Empire 31, 32
William Ellis 98
Winston Churchill 37
  Blood, Toil, Tears and Sweat 175
World War One 109, 118, 142, 143, 150
  First World War 127, 142

World War Two 122, 123, 137
  Second World War 156
Wu Zetian 10, 40, 41, 42, 44, 45, 46, 47,
    48, 55, 61, 65
  Book of Tang 44
  China 40, 41, 44, 48
  Chinese dynasty 41
  Chinese history 44
  Emperor Taizong 42
  Empress Consort 41
  Empress Regent 48
  Empress Wang 43
  Gaozong 42, 43
  Li Dan 43, 44
  Li Jingye 44, 45
  Liu Binwang 46
  Li Xian 43, 44
  Lue Binwang 44, 45
  Mandarin 41
  Shizicong 42
  Taizong 42, 43
  Tang dynasty 41, 55
  Wu 40, 41, 42, 43, 44, 45, 46, 47, 48
  Wu Tse-tien and other Politics of Legitimation in T'ang China) 44
  Wu Zhou Dynasty 41

Y

Yad Vashem 144
  The World Holocaust Remembrance Centre 144

Z

zoomorphic ad hominem 200
Zoomorphic imagery 46

ACKNOWLEDGEMENTS

There are many people who need thanks and acknowledgement for the production of this book.

First and foremost, I have to thank my old school history teacher Nicolas Kinloch, who sparked my love of history when I was 11. When I started researching for this book, I reached out to Nicolas who, despite the many years that had passed, was still happy to offer mentorship to his former pupil. Many of the chapters in this book were only possible thanks to the knowledge he was willing to share. Nicolas remains to this day one of the finest historians I knew. Whether it was Madagascar, China, Mongolia, or Nazi Germany, he seemed to know everything about every speech ever given.

When we sat down for coffee in Cambridge and I told him about the book, he started reeling off momentous speeches and obscure historical figures that needed to be included. He paused at one point, gave me a stern look, and said, 'Guy, I want you to know that I expect a grovelling acknowledgement'. Known for his dramatic style, Nicolas decided to die a few months before this book was due to be published, and he never got to read the final work to which he contributed so much.

My thanks also go to Martin Hickman and Gaby Monteiro from Canbury Press for all of the support they gave me in the production of the book and their direction and patience. I also received immeasurable support from my wonderful literary agency, CMM – thank you to Lisa, Zoe and Jamie for all of your help, guidance and support.

My entire fascination into the world of rhetoric and speeches would never have happened were it not for the Department of Classics at Royal Holloway. My fascination for speeches was sparked during a second year module on logic and rhetoric led by Professor Jonathan Powell and his amazing colleagues at the Centre for Oratory and Rhetoric. On the subject of rhetoric and speeches, I also have to thank my speechwriting colleagues from the European Speechwriter Network who helped me break into the profession when I was a recent graduate, and taught me most of what I know.

When writing this book, I received help from many friends, colleagues and – in some cases – strangers, who helped form various chapters: for Napoleon, I would like to thank Anne Theurier; for Eva Perón, I would like to thank Lucas Rodd; for Caesar, I would like to thank Henriette van der Blom from the University of Birmingham whose research and willingness to help aided greatly; for Wu, I would like to thank the various sinologists at the University of Cambridge who helped me hunt for sources, as well as Professor Richard Guisso from the University of Toronto who allowed me to use one of his excellent translations; and, finally, for the chapter on Catherine the Great which didn't make it into the final manuscript, I would like to thank the team at UCL's School of Slavonic and Eastern European

Studies, particularly Professor Pamela Davidson, who directed me towards sources.

I also received a lot of support from the illustrious Dr Yair Doza (aka dad) who, despite being a biochemist, is an avid history enthusiast.

Thanks also go to the keen-eyed Dr Toby Parsloe who helped eradicate many typographical errors from both this book and also my first book *How to Apologise for Killing a Cat: Rhetoric and the Art of Persuasion*.

GUY DOZA

Guy Doza is a speechwriter, trainer, and public affairs consultant. He started his career in political research before branching out into corporate speechwriting. He now works independently for a range of international clients whom he writes on a variety of subjects. Guy is a two-time TEDx speaker and has lectured on rhetoric at several of the world's leading universities.

His first book is **How to Apologise for Killing a Cat: Rhetoric and the Art of Persuasion** (Canbury Press, 2022).

More titles from Canbury Press

How to Apologise for Killing a Cat
Rhetoric and the Art of Persuasion
Guy Doza
ISBN: 9781912454709

'Most books on persuasion teach the few how to sway the many. With wit and vim, Guy has given us something else: an X-ray into the tactics of those trying to change our minds and behaviour.'
Stephen Krupin, former speechwriter for Barack Obama

More titles from Canbury Press

Zelensky
A Biography of Ukraine's War Leader
Steven Derix
ISBN: 9781912454778

Zelensky is the first major biography of Ukraine's leader written for a Western audience.

Publish with Us

Do you have an idea for a book?

Contact us at **submissions@canburypress.com**

www.canburypress.com

info@canburypress.com